Fishing
THE
Salmon
River

Fishing
THE
Salmon
River

An Angler's Guide to the Famed New York State Fishery

Spider Rybaak

Burford Books

Photography by Roman Hrynyk

Printed in the United States of America

10 9 8 7 6 5 4 3 2 1

Library of Congress Cataloging-in-Publication Data
is on file with the Library of Congress

DEDICATION

To Susan

CERTAINTY

Spring blushes into bloom
Summer burns away
autumn colors swirl
winter's white and grey

Some blame God
others don't dare
no one knows
you don't care.

Just come
and go
bringing
cool warmth
hot heat
warm cold
and snow.

Roman Hrynyk

SEEKING CHROME

Climbing icy rapids
over trembling logs
glistening webs of line
and pieces of Styrofoam
glued to the rocks
waving
straining
against sparkling welds
of frozen foam.

Wedges of beaten floes
lucid and hard
like shattered dreams
grind against the hope
of raising a rainbow
through fragmented light.

Roman Hrynyk

Salmon River Falls in winter.

Acknowledgments

Without the help of the following folks this book would only be a dream: Karen "Bubblez" Ashley, Bob Barker, Sue Bookhout, Susan Douglass, Brian Eisch, Sue Ennis, Gary Fischer, Walt Geryk, John Hrynyk, Walter Hrynyk, John Kopy, Fred Kucharski, Malinda's Fly, Tackle and Spey Shop, Michael McGrath II, Capt. Richard Miick, Dave Oulette, Mabel Oulette, Stan Oulette, John Rucando, Captain Richard Stanton, Walter Tarnawsky, Fran Verdoliva, Steve Wiatrak, LaVern Williams, Dave Woods, Jack Zasada.

Contents

Introduction

Capable of swimming great distances against raging rapids, able to leap tall waterfalls with a single bound, engaging in arm-wrenching battles when hooked, salmon have been swimming through Western man's imagination ever since he first set eyes on them. Ancient Romans fished for them with flies tied of dyed wool, in the streams of what would someday be known as England. Vikings swept over Europe with smoked salmon on their breaths.

The Old World only had one species: Atlantic salmon. Its flesh and caviar were in such high demand that the species was extirpated from most European rivers by the time Columbus set sail for America. The few, isolated populations that remained were protected and set aside for royalty. Commoners caught poaching them were treated harshly.

Free of the environmental damage Western civilization wrought on the continent over the millennia, America was a different story. When the first Europeans arrived in the northeast, they were delighted to find that the streams draining into Lake Ontario and the Atlantic Ocean hosted massive runs of Atlantic salmon. They were so plentiful in the smallest Great Lake, in fact, that several of its tributaries are named after them. The most famous is the Salmon River.

A combination of over-fishing (they were dried and burned for fuel in ships, farmers used them for fertilizer), pollution, and, most importantly, milldams blocking their way to spawning grounds proved more than the Atlantic salmon could take, and all but wiped them out of Lake Ontario by the end of the 19th century. Miraculously, a few survived into the 1960s, creating quite a stir whenever one was shown off in waterfront taverns from Buffalo to Watertown (some say these fish originated in the Finger Lakes).

Its greatest predator removed from the scene, Lake Ontario's alewife population exploded. By the mid-60s, its beaches were lined with windrows of dead baitfish 18 inches high by three feet wide.

Unsightly, crunchy under foot, casting a terrible stench to boot, the tiny cadavers spurred beach-goers, waterfront owners and the new breed of vocal environmentalists spawned by the hippie movement to demand remediation. The state responded by stocking the lake's largest feeders, particularly the Salmon River, with some of the aquatic world's most voracious appetites: Pacific salmon, steelhead and brown trout.

Finding their new haunts agreeable, the salmonids moved right in, tearing into the schools of bait like kids into cake, easily growing to trophy proportions: kings averaging 16 pounds and coho a cool eight. In September, 1989, a 33 lb. 4 oz. coho—a species indigenous to the Pacific Ocean, no less—was caught in the Salmon River, breaking the world record, and putting Pulaski, NY, on the map as one of the world's premier fishing destinations.

Recognizing a steady source of revenue and good PR when they see it, the power company and state went to work making the stream as fisherman-friendly as possible. Public access sites with parking, some with drift-boat launches, sprang up all along the river. The Pine Grove boat launch, a dual-ramped facility for motorized craft, complete with parking for 120 rigs, was built on the south shore within sight of the mouth, a bass and pike hot spot locals call the Estuary.

While public access is plentiful on the 17 miles of the lower river, its banks aren't totally free. Fishing is prohibited around the hatchery. Additionally, the first mile or so of water open to fishing below the dam is restricted to fly-fishing only. In other words, fly-fishing is allowed on any part of the river that's open to angling, but fishing with bait and lures is prohibited from the Altmar bridge upstream to the no fishing sign in the gorge below the Lighthouse Hill Reservoir dam.

Additionally, the Douglaston Salmon Run, a private operation, charges a fee to fish from shore or by wading the two-something-miles of water it controls: the south bank downstream from the Jefferson Street Bridge in Pulaski; and both banks about 100 yards downstream of the Black Hole to a few hundred feet above the NY 3 Bridge.

Keep in mind, the DSR can only post its property: the river's banks and floor. Since no one owns the water, float-fishing from a tube, kayak, drift boat, you name it, is permitted; but you can't anchor or step out of the craft.

Below the DSR runs a watery web called the "Estuary." Mainly marsh with channels running through it, it's difficult to fish from shore. The state built a public fishing access site on the north channel, right off NY 3.

Spring sees lake-run perch in the eight- to 12-inch range, bullheads over a foot long, and black crappies the size of small frying pans storm the Estuary, congregating in massive schools from the lighthouse to the Trailer Hole (an abandoned trailer on the north bank marks the spot), the first deep hole upstream of the NY 3 Bridge. Sunfish and rock bass thrive in the slow flow from late April to the end of August when the sight of early running salmon send them beating fins for the big pond.

Lake-run smallmouths spawn in the rapids all the way up to the Lighthouse Hill Reservoir dam. Finding the relatively warm, caressing currents and bait-rich pools, runs and channels to their liking, many stay until the first salmon run them out in mid-August. Indeed, before salmon were introduced into the system in the late '60s, Selkirk was nationally famous for trophy bass.

Northern pike occupy the Estuary's weed edges and channels—the closer to the lighthouse the better.

Glamorous gamefish and tasty panfish aren't this stretch of the stream's only claims to fame—it offers low-lifes, too. In spring, bull-heads pour into the lower river, offering great evening entertainment for bank-anglers gathered under the warm glow of lanterns and camp-fires. Autumn finds monster catfish foraging on the floor from the lighthouse to the mouth.

The Salmon River ranks as one of the world's great fisheries, boasting two major records to prove it: the Great Lakes record chinook salmon (47 lbs. 13 oz.) and the world record coho salmon (33 lbs. 4 oz.); a species native to the Pacific Ocean, no less.

A river for all ages, this fabulous, 44-mile-long stream does it all, fulfilling dreams ranging from a child's desire for a mess of panfish to an aging angler's fantasy wall-hanger. It's the perfect place to cast your hopes for a trophy the size of the one swimming around in your dreams.

PART I

GETTING TO KNOW THE SALMON RIVER

Ethics

Fighting a trophy trout or salmon can be intoxicating. Some guys get so worked up they lose their senses, becoming blind to the crowd around them. Standing firm, rod high in the air, they allow the fish to run, crossing every line in its path, then wonder why everyone's getting angry at them. . . . Here's what you need to know.

The first thing to do when you hook a fish is to yell "fish on," so those around you can get out of the way.

Put as little space between you and the fish as possible. If you're in a pool, follow it upstream and downstream. If you're in rapids, chase after it until you reach a pocket where the two of you can tug at each other without getting in everyone's way.

Land the fish as quickly as possible. When it wants to run, set your drag as tight as you dare, raise your rod high and let it go. When it tires, pump it in.

If you plan on releasing it, unhook it in the water.

If you want to take a hero shot first, pull the fish as close to you as possible and wait for it to stop thrashing. Wet your hands to avoid removing slime and scales. Moving slowly, grab the tail with one hand, cradle its belly or jaw with the other and gently lift it horizontally. Take the photo and let it go.

Pacific salmon are a proud breed and won't take much abuse. They don't survive out of water for very long, and don't cotton to stringers, dying quickly, especially if you move them around a lot.

Don't forget the human element. It's a good idea to practice patience toward your fellow man when fishing a world famous hot spot like this. During salmon time, there are a lot of out-of-towners on the river; many are experienced, but some aren't. For a lot of the newbies, it's a major lifetime event. Having saved for years to make the trip, they'll do just about anything for a salmon. Be patient. Follow the golden rule so that everyone has good memories.

Tug Hill Weather

Springing out of the Tug Hill plateau—one of the most remote regions of the state—the Salmon River is squeaky clean. In fact, the Lewis

County town of Osceola, the source of the river's east and west forks, and the Oswego County town of Redfield, birthplace of the North Branch, make national news each winter with their massive snowfalls. Similarly, these counties are soaked with copious rain in warm weather. This steady precipitation keeps the river high and relatively cool during the peak salmon and trout runs, early fall through spring.

Danger: Rising Water

Used to be, the hydro plant could generate power whenever it wanted to, often sending wading anglers hilariously slipping and sliding for the bank. Not anymore. Now-a-days, the facility can only release water at night when fishing on the lower river is prohibited.

When the power company isn't interfering with its flow, the Salmon River rises and falls with the seasons. Winter and summer see the stream sliding over the landscape in a series of gentle rapids punctuated with long, deep pools. Anglers can wade it in hip boots, and even cross it in spots.

Spring and fall are a different story. Winter's thaw, autumn rains and drawdown turn the river into a series of long, raging rapids broken by short stretches of quiet water in the biggest pools.

Before you go cursing the power company for interfering with the natural order, bear in mind that generating electricity isn't the only reason water is released by the utility. Supporting the river's aquatic life forms, spurring mature salmonids upstream to the hatchery and natural spawning grounds, and keeping the river high enough for egg incubation bear equal weight.

Regular daily releases vary with the seasons. The minimum volume, also called summer base flow (May 1 to August 31), is 185 cubic feet per second. Volume is increased to 335 cfs from September 1 to December 31; and is dropped to 285 cfs from January 1 through April 30.

Additionally, the power company releases water for recreational purposes like kayaking five times each summer: one 400 cfs release in June; one 750 cfs release in August and on Labor Day; and two 750 cfs releases in July.

"Base flows are determined to protect anglers, too," says Fran Verdoliva, New York State Department of Environmental Conservation's Special Assistant for the Salmon River. "If there's a surplus of water in the reservoir, the power company generally releases it at night when fishing on the lower river is prohibited."

Don't be discouraged by the river's notorious "rising water." If you'd rather fish when the water is low, morning is your best time— relatively speaking, of course (in spring, the river stays high all day long). While it can be a real pain if it starts rising and you're out in the middle, forcing you to high-tail it for the bank, high water makes the fish more aggressive.

The rising river has a lot of space to fill en route to Lake Ontario. Here's how long it takes to reach some popular spots:

Altmar: 30 minutes

Pineville: 1 hour 40 minutes

Interstate 81: 2 hours 50 minutes

Black Hole: 3 hours 30 minutes

For the day's water levels, call Brookfield Renewable Power's Waterline, 1-800-452-1742 and enter sign-code 365123.

Still, you gotta be careful. The river drains a large watershed, roughly 280 square miles. It takes a while for storm run-off on the Tug Hill Plateau to reach the lower river, and the water can come up without warning. Additionally, it can be sunny in Pulaski, raining in Redfield. **If you're wading the lower river, make a mental note of an object in the water (tree, boulder, bridge abutment, bank) and if the river begins rising on it, head for shore immediately.**

If rapids ain't your thing, no sweat. A few big holes slow the flow regardless of water level, offering relatively peaceful settings during periods of heavy run-off: Pulaski's Railroad Bridge, Long and Short Bridge Pools and Black Hole, for instance, and the Sportsmens and Trestle Pools, downstream and upstream, respectively, of Pineville.

Stocking Statistics

Upstream of Redfield, the NYSDEC treats the Salmon River like any other trout stream, stocking it in May. The numbers are pretty much the same from year to year: The main stem gets 840 brook trout and 1150 rainbow trout ranging from eight to nine inches, while the North Branch gets 3020 brookies the same size.

Fish aren't stocked between the impoundments. Above the falls, located half-way between the reservoirs, the water is too warm in summer to support trout.

Downstream of the cataract springs pouring off the gorge rim keep the water cool enough to draw—and hold—trout from the lower reservoir. Incidentally, the plunge pool is loaded with smallmouth bass running from six to 14 inches.

The final 16-mile-stretch of river, from Lighthouse Hill Reservoir to the mouth, gets the lion's share of human intervention. The authorities ensure this section lives up to its reputation as a world class fishery by stocking salmonids annually; mostly Pacific varieties raised in the state-of-the-art hatchery in Altmar.

According to Verdoliva, whose office is in the building, each year the facility releases about 350,000 chinook salmon, 90,000 coho salmon, 120,000 Chamber Creek (winter-run) steelhead and 48,000 Skamania (summer-run) steelhead. When stocking time comes around, fingerling and yearling salmon and trout are released into the hatchery's smolt release pond which drains, via the hatchery's fish ladder, into Beaverdam Brook, a tributary of the Salmon River. These fish are all raised from eggs and milt taken from fish that return to the facility.

About 60,000 Atlantic salmon are stocked into the river, behind the hatchery, annually. The USGS's Tunison Labs in Cortland contributes 30,000, and another 30,000 come from the NYSDEC's Adirondack hatchery.

"Surplus brown trout from various state hatcheries, including 1,000 two-year-olds, are released at several locations along the river," says Verdoliva, adding: "They're the only species that's stocked for immediate harvest. All but the browns should be released, unless, of course, you catch a trophy."

Best Times to Fish

Upstream of the Salmon River Reservoir, and in the short stretch running between the falls and the lower reservoir, the fish are year-round residents, behaving like trout do in any other blue-ribbon stream, feeding best about an hour on either side of dawn and dusk, especially in May and June, September through October 15. In addition, a light rain—just enough to dimple the surface—often triggers a bite.

Below Lighthouse Hill Reservoir, the river boasts seasonal runs of lake-run species so the best time to fish depends on the species you're after.

The stream's namesakes, Atlantic salmon, for instance, spawn earlier than Pacific varieties. The most warmwater-tolerant of the species, small groups of landlocks enter the rapids as early as April and continue running into November.

August finds massive quantities of Pacific salmon milling around in the lake off the sticks—the piers at the mouth of the river. They come in close enough at night for anglers to head out into the lake off the mouth in rowboats, anchor and still-fish for them on bottom, using gobs of salmon roe for bait.

Mid-September sparks the main run. Some days see so many kings and coho charge upstream, locals claim the river rises a couple of inches. Their numbers start dwindling by mid-October and the run comes to an end in November.

The lake's resident brown trout run the same time the Pacific salmon do. Popularly called football browns, they end up stealing the show for many visiting anglers who never saw browns that big before.

Steelhead are always in the river. The Washington strain is the most common. Autumn sees massive numbers follow in the wakes of the salmon and browns to feed on their eggs. Sharing the rapids with salmon twice their size makes chromers extremely aggressive.

When the salmon run is over, fresh steelhead continue trickling into the stream all winter long to feast on their eggs. Come spring, the Chamber Creek strain runs the snow-melt swollen rapids in mass to spawn, and Skamania (summer steelhead) follow in summer.

From the lower reservoir upstream, trout season runs from April 1 through October 15. Only two trout of the five fish daily limit can be longer than 12 inches. In Redfield Reservoir, trout season is year-round, and only two of the five fish daily limit can be longer than 12 inches.

In late spring, smallmouth bass and northern pike rule the marshy area downstream of the NY 3 Bridge and respond to their usual favorites: minnows, jigs and crankbaits; the bronzebacks take crayfish, too. Come August, water temperatures usually rise to unbearable levels, forcing most back into the lake.

Yellow perch are in the Estuary all year long, and are especially popular in deep summer when they're about all you can count on to bite.

Channel catfish, drawn by the scent of salmon cadavers, storm the channel downstream of the lighthouse in September and October.

Bullheads run the marshy areas of the Estuary in spring to spawn.

Fish Consumption Advisory

While eating fish is generally considered good for you, the state's waters have all been corrupted to some degree by pollution and the authorities recommend women under 50 years of age and children under 15 eat no fish taken from the Lower Salmon River.

Everyone else is advised to limit consumption of smallmouth bass, white perch and white suckers of any size, brown trout over 20 inches, and lake trout over 25 inches to one, 8-ounce meal per month.

Brown trout smaller than 20 inches, lake trout shorter than 25 inches and all other fish not mentioned above can be eaten up to four times a month.

Carp and channel catfish shouldn't be eaten at all.

For a printed copy of the state's detailed "Health Advice on Eating Sportfish and Game," or electronic updates on the health advisory, go to www.health.ny.gov/fish.

Popular Baits

Only one hook with a single point is permitted, except for floating lures and flies (see the section on "Special Regulations for Great Lakes Tributaries" in the Freshwater Fishing Guide). Salted minnows are effective for steelhead and browns in rapids most anytime.

One of Lake Ontario's greatest spawning grounds, the Salmon River is a fish factory. Its most important raw material is fish eggs, especially salmon and trout varieties. They're the most popular bait, too, because just about everything in the drink feeds on them. In fact, they're what draws steelhead into the river in the fall and winter.

Some anglers prefer trout eggs, claiming they're more productive than salmon eggs. However, it's illegal to sell them in the state, so you'll have to catch a mature female brown or rainbow and provide your own.

Some of the most successful guides on the river carry the oldest bait in the book, the lowly night crawler, as a last resort. Worms work well spring through autumn, and during winter thaws, when the water is murky and high. Brace yourself for countless fallfish and creek minnows between trout during the warm months.

A 6 mm bead (imitates an egg) fished below a float is one of the best baits on the river. Tied above the hook, you seldom lose them to snags—the knot at the hook usually breaks first. What's more, the material they're made from is usually impervious to teeth. Hard and soft varieties are available.

While many anglers fish with a single salmon egg (artificial or cured), most prefer egg sacs: clumps of roe or several eggs wrapped in mesh (fine, net-like material) to about the size of a marble. Local bait shops sell them, as well as the stuff to make them.

Curiously (they're supposed to stop feeding when they enter the river), salmon strike egg sacs. In fact, it's the most common bait used to target fish staging at the mouth of the river before running upstream. While no one really knows why (and the salmon ain't talkin'), several theories exist. The most popular suggests they destroy the spawn of others to enhance the survival of their own. Another theory argues they still have the urge to feed but their stomachs can only take liquid diets like fish eggs.

Swinging a streamer like a wooly bugger through the current (casting across the river and letting the current swing the fly downstream through the rapids) is a good idea any time, even on the coldest winter days. Trout usually hit at the end of the drift, when the offering turns abruptly at the current's edge and faces upstream. The best colors are chartreuse and brown.

Yarn flies resembling salmon eggs are the most popular patterns on the river, especially in winter. They're typically fished on bottom in fast water; or suspended deep, below floats, in pools.

One of the most recent additions to a well-dressed Salmon River anglers' fly box is the Polish woven nymph. Green and brown versions are the most popular.

In-line spinners like Mepps Aglias and Worden's Rooster Tails are productive, even in deep winter, especially at the tails of pools. Keep them small, ⅛ oz. or less.

Crankbaits like Flatfish, Hot n' tots and Rapalas are productive for casting, drifting and back trolling.

Dry flies sometimes trigger bites on sunny, windless days, late spring through mid-autumn. One of fishing's greatest thrills is seeing a monster steelhead rise to a fly.

A juicy piece of salmon is the best bait for monster catfish in the river's mouth. "Cut bait is legal" says NYSDEC's Dave Lemon, "so long as it was legally caught that same day from the same body of water, and was counted towards the limit for that species."

Catch and Release

One thing all competent anglers with average luck can expect to do on the Salmon River and its reservoirs is catch fish. So many, in fact, some will have to be released eventually for reasons ranging from the fish being out of season or too small, to catching more than you need or simply practicing catch and release. Whatever the reason, it is in the best interests of all concerned for the critter to be released unharmed. Here are some simple pointers to ensure you release a fish with a future instead of a dead fish swimming:

- Don't go after trophy browns and steelhead with ultralight tackle. While it may be fun for you, the futile struggle for escape can exhaust the fish beyond recovery.
- Only use a net when absolutely necessary. Nets tear mouths, rip gills, break fins and teeth, scratch eyes, and remove slime, an important barrier against harmful bacteria.
- Keep the fish submerged in water, even when unhooking it.
- If you must remove a fish from the water, always wet your hands before touching it, and place it on something wet and soft, like leaves, for instance.

- If the fish is hooked deep in the tongue, guts, or gills, cut the line. Fish are bleeders, and an internal wound as small as a pinhole can be fatal. By leaving the hook in place, healing can occur around it as it rusts away.
- Never lift a pike by squeezing its eyes with your fingers.
- Keep fingers out of a fish's gills.

Essentials

If you fish exclusively from shore, and don't mind breaking off even when the line is snagged only an arm's reach away, in water just a couple of feet deep, any ol' footgear will do. However, you're going to run into moments—often several times a day, in fact—when you'll need to wade in to cast out a little further, land a fish, or get to the other side. Pouring off the Tug Hill Plateau, the river packs a powerful current, and is exceptionally slippery. Anglers are advised to wear boots with studded traction devices like Korkers (felt soles are inadequate), and carry a wading staff—even when the river is down.

Personal Flotation Devices

Besides being exceptionally slippery, the Salmon River's water level constantly changes, sometimes a couple of times a day. If you plan on crossing or fishing out in the middle, it's a good idea to have a personal flotation device handy in case you fall in, especially in cold weather when frigid water temperatures can cause numbness, making movement difficult.

Invasive Species

Spiny water fleas, zebra mussels, water chestnut, round goby . . . it seems every year introduces a new critter into the Great Lakes anglers' lexicon. Unfortunately, exotic species hurt: they hurt fish by destroying habitat and competing for scarce food sources; they hurt anglers by fouling fishing spots and equipment; and they hurt the outdoors by altering the environment. Anglers can help prevent the spread of invasive species by following these simple steps:

- Remove all mud, plants, fish or animals from equipment before leaving the access site.
- Remove water from equipment like live wells and bait buckets before leaving the site.
- Clean and dry boats, trailers, boots and anything else that came into contact with the water.
- Never release a fish or discard a plant into a body of water unless it came from there.
- Wear traction devices made of metal instead of carpet or felt.

Sturgeon Alert

The state's attempt to restore lake sturgeon into the Great Lakes system is bearing fruit. Anglers are catching increasing numbers of four-something-footers, particularly in the large tributaries in spring. Although its size, shark-like appearance and bony plates make it look tough, it's still a fish and shouldn't be handled. Females can take up to 26 years to reach reproductive age—males mature in half that time—and they only spawn about every six years. Lake sturgeon are totally protected, and it is illegal to target them or possess them. If you catch one and just gotta photograph it, take its picture while it's in the water, then release it immediately.

Regulations

The following special regulation governs the river and its reservoirs from its headwaters to the Lighthouse Hill Reservoir Dam:

- No more than two trout in the five-fish daily limit can be longer than 12 inches.

Redfield Reservoir has special regulations:
- Trout can be taken all year.
- Minimum size for walleye is 18 inches.
- Daily limit for walleye is three.

Salmon River feeding Redfield Reservoir in summer.

From the Lighthouse Hill Reservoir dam to the mouth, the river claims a whole page in the "New York Freshwater Fishing Regulations Guide." It's located in the "Special Regulations for Great Lakes Tributaries," under "Special Regulations by Section for Salmon River and Tributaries (Oswego County)."

Public Fishing Rights

The state owns public fishing rights (permanent easements giving anglers the right to walk and fish) on most of the river, including 12 miles of the lower stream (from the no-fishing zone upstream of the fly-fishing-only section in Altmar to the Douglaston Salmon Run in Pulaski). PFRs are marked with yellow signs announcing "Public Fishing Stream," nailed to trees. Access is limited to the streambed and a 33-foot wide band of river bank; activities other than fishing are prohibited. (For detailed maps of the PFR, go to: www.dec.ny.gov/docs/fish_marine_pdf/r7salrivpfr.pdf)

Definitions (Glossary)

ANGLING: According to the NYSDEC: "Angling means taking fish by hook and line. This includes bait and fly fishing, casting, trolling and the use of landing nets to complete the catch. Anglers must be in immediate attendance when their lines are in the water. Snatching, lifting, hooking and use of tip-ups are not angling."

ATLANTICS: landlocked Atlantic salmon.

BREAKLINES: A steep drop from shallow to deep water.

BLACK BASS: Largemouth and smallmouth bass.

BROWNS: Brown trout.

BUCKEYE: Emerald shiner.

BONEY: Shallow and rocky.

CENTERPIN: Specifically designed for floatfishing, a centerpin reel looks like a regular fly reel but is open at the arbor on one side so line comes off easily during the cast—like an open-face spinning reel— only sideways. A clicker is its only drag so the angler has to palm it while fighting a fish.

CLEAN FISH: Salmonids free of wounds caused by lampreys or snaggers.

CONTROLLED DRIFT: Using oars or a trolling motor to control the speed and direction of a drift.

CHROMER: Steelhead.

CHUCK-N'-DUCK: Using weight, usually split-shot, with fly-fishing equipment.

COMBAT FISHING: Angling shoulder-to-shoulder during the run, usually on weekends.

CURLY-TAIL: Soft plastic grub, a.k.a. twister tail

CUT-BAIT: Pieces of salmon with skin attached (usually bellies) used to catch kings just off the river's mouth in late summer, and catfish the rest of the year.

DARTER: A cigar-shaped surface plug that darts from side to side.

DBL: Drift boat launch.

DEC: The state's Department of Environmental Conservation.

DSR: Douglaston Salmon Run

DRIFT BOAT (MCKENZIE BOAT): Built with an arched bottom (so it spins easily in rapids), steep sides and a flat floor, this craft was developed on Oregon's McKenzie River for fishing in whitewater.

DRIFT FISHING OR FLOAT TRIP: 1. Floating downstream with the current, lures running off the back of the boat, and slapping the water with your oars just enough to slow the boat down a skoosh and give the plugs some action. 2. Floating down river and anchoring periodically to fish.

DROP BACK: Trout that has spawned and is returning to the lake.

ECO: Environmental Conservation officer.

EGG SAC: The most popular bait on the river, it's made by wrapping several salmon or trout eggs in fine mesh to about the size of a marble.

ESTUARY: The marshy lower river stretching from the last set of rapids to the last bend, a couple of hundred yards upstream of the lighthouse.

FAS: Fishing access site.

FISHING ON THE FLY: Casting from a moving drift boat, often while the guide is rowing.

FLATLINE: Trolling with the lure attached directly to the main line, and without additional weight.

FLATWING STREAMER: A streamer tied so the wing hugs the body and rides horizontally, like a black ghost.

FLOAT (BOBBER) FISHING: Using a float to keep your bait at a desired depth, and to help in detecting strikes.

FLY BOOK: A book-like container used to hold artificial flies.

FLY-FISHING: Using a heavy line and long rod to cast artificial flies made of light-weight materials like animal hair, feathers, yarn and thread.

FREELINE: Fishing a bait, usually a minnow, without added weight.

FRESH FISH: Fish that just entered the river from the lake.

GLO BUG: An egg pattern fly.

HYDRAULIC: Boil-like backwash created when water pours over structure and recirculates.

JACKS: Male kings that mature in two years.

JENNIES: Female kings that mature in two years.

KAMIKAZE CAST: Casting into a pool lined on both sides with anglers.

KING: Chinook salmon.

LOWER RIVER: The stretch from Lighthouse Hill Reservoir dam to the mouth.

MINNOWBAIT: Hard, minnow-imitating crankbait like a Thunderstick or Bass Pro Shops XPS Extreme Minnow.

NYSDEC OR DEC: New York State Department of Environmental Conservation.

PANFISH: This category includes bluegills, pumpkinseeds, yellow perch, rock bass and bullheads; relatively easy to catch, one of these tasty little critters is usually an angler's first fish.

PAS: Public Access Site.

PIKEASAURUS: Northern pike.

ROW-TROLLING: Trolling by rowing.

SKAMANIA: Summer-running steelhead.

SLINKY: Snag resistant weight system in which split shots are inserted into a nylon cord.

SMALLIES: Smallmouth bass.

SNATCHING OR SNAGGING: Foul hooking fish intentionally.

SPEY CASTING: A fly-fishing technique developed on Scotland's River Spey, a 12- to 15-foot long rod (also called the double-handed fly rod) and heavy fly line are used to cast flies up to 80 feet, even in the wind. The technique involves feeding line equalling the distance to your target into the stream. Using a backcast, send the line behind you, then, with a flick of the wrist, point the rod tip at the target and whip the fly forward.

STREAMER: A large fly tied to resemble a minnow; typically swung through current or retrieved through pools.

STICKWORM: Fat plastic worm like a Senko or YUM Dinger.

THE RUN: Autumn's salmon migration.

THE STICKS: Piers at the mouth of the Salmon River.

WALK-THE-DOG: Jerking a darter so its head swings from side to side.

WHITEWATER: Rapids.

Fish Species of the Salmon River

BROOK TROUT A.K.A. SPECKLED TROUT AND NATIVES (*Salvelinus frontinalis*)

GENERAL DESCRIPTION: This colorful fish boasts a labyrinthine pattern of worm-like markings on its dark olive back, large light spots speckled with tiny red ones (some circled in blue) on its sides, an orange belly and lower fins—the forward edges of the lower fins are lined in white. A member of the char family, its mouth and appetite are greater than your average trout's.

ADDITIONAL INFORMATION: Mostly found in the upper river and its tributaries, mature males have hooked jaws. Its propensity for eagerly striking just about anything that moves and fits in its mouth—worms, minnows, crayfish, flies, spoons, spinners, jigs, you name it—earns it the distinction of being the easiest trout to catch. The state's official fish and smallest trout, most range from four to10 inches long; 18-something inchers are possible. The NYSDEC stocks 840 annually into the river upstream of Redfield. The state record, caught in the Silver Lake Wilderness Area of the Adirondack Mountains by Richard Beauchamp on May 16, 2013, is six pounds.

BROWN TROUT (*Salmo trutta*)

GENERAL DESCRIPTION: Sporting deep, brown backs, this species' color lightens into golden sides splashed with red and brown spots surrounded by light halos. Sometimes the red spots are so bright they look like burning embers. Mature males sport kypes (curved lower jaws) that are often hooked so extremely they seem deformed.

ADDITIONAL INFORMATION: Imported in the 1830s from Germany, browns found America to their liking and have prospered. Far more tolerant of warm water than brookies or lakers, they do well in every kind of clean, oxygenated water, from deep lakes to shallow streams. Purist fly-fishermen consider the brown the savviest of trout. Its propensity for hitting a well presented dry fly has endeared it with some of the world's most famous authors, Dame Julianna Berners, Issac Walton, William Butler Yeats and Ernest Hemingway, to name a few. Especially colorful when they spawn in autumn, about the same time as Pacific salmon, browns are a fitting complement to the earth's most beautiful season. The state record, caught in Lake Ontario on June 10, 1997, by Tony Brown (no relation), weighed 33 pounds, 2 ounces.

STEELHEAD AND RAINBOW TROUT (*Oncorhynchus mykiss*)

GENERAL DESCRIPTION: This species has a deep green back which melts into silvery sides. A pink stripe stretching from the corner of the fish's jaw to the base of its tail is what gives it its name. The upper half of its body, its upper fins and the entire tail are splattered with irregular black spots.

ADDITIONAL INFORMATION: Native to the West Coast, rainbows were introduced to New York in the 19th century (called domestic rainbows, descendants of these pioneers are mostly found in the upper river and North Branch). Steelhead, the anadromous form, was introduced into the lake late in the last century. Averaging eight pounds, often growing over 20 pounds, it's the most popular fish on the river. Steelies spend the warm months in the big pond, running upstream in autumn, in the wakes of salmon and brown trout to feast on their eggs. Finding the pickings good, many stay all winter. Come spring, they're joined by fresh fish from the lake that run upriver to spawn. Unlike salmon, they survive, returning to spawn again, sometimes several times, over multiple years. Recently, the DEC has been stocking Skamania, a summer-running strain. The state record, caught in Lake Ontario by Robert Wilson on August 14, 2004, tipped the scale at 31 pounds, 3 ounces.

ATLANTIC SALMON A.K.A. LANDLOCKED SALMON (*Salmo salar*)

GENERAL DESCRIPTION: The only salmon native to the state, they generally have deep brown backs which quickly brighten to silvery sides sprinkled with irregularly shaped spots which are often crossed.

Closely resembling Pacific salmon, you can tell them apart by counting the rays in their anal fin: Atlantics have 12 or less.

ADDITIONAL INFORMATION: At one time, Lake Ontario boasted the greatest population of landlocked Atlantic salmon in the world. A combination of pollution, dams on natal streams, and sterility caused by a vitamin B1 deficiency linked to eating exotic forage (alewives and smelt), wiped them out. Currently, the DEC maintains a token presence by stocking fingerlings regularly. In addition, local, state, and federal agencies chip in by unloading surplus fish from hatcheries and research laboratories. *Salmo Salar* (the leaper in Latin) is the only salmon to survive the spawning ordeal, often returning to do the deed a second time—sometimes even a third. Considered the classiest salmon, catching one on a fly is many a fly-fishing purist's greatest dream. Atlantics spawn in November. The state record, caught in Lake Ontario on April 5, 1997, weighed 24 pounds, 15 ounces.

Landing a king in downtown Pulaski.

CHINOOK SALMON A.K.A. KING SALMON (*Oncorhynchus tshawytscha*)

GENERAL DESCRIPTION: A silvery fish with a green back, it has black spots along the upper half of its body, including the fins and the entire tail. When ready to spawn, its back becomes dark green to olive brown. The inside of the mouth is entirely black; males develop a kype (hooked jaw).

ADDITIONAL INFORMATION: The largest of the Pacific salmon, kings were introduced into Lake Ontario in the late 1960s. Easily reaching 35 pounds, they're one of the lake's most important game fish. The most exciting fishing occurs mid-September through October, when mature, 3.5-year-olds averaging 25 pounds, and precocious 1.5 year-olds averaging eight pounds, run the river to spawn, dying soon afterwards. The state record, caught in the Salmon River on September 7, 1991, weighed 47 pounds, 13 ounces.

COHO SALMON A.K.A. SILVER SALMON (*Oncorhynchus kisutch*)

GENERAL DESCRIPTION: Another Pacific salmon, the coho is a silvery fish when actively feeding in the lake but develops a wide, red stripe on its sides when it stops eating and heads upstream to spawn. The upper half of its body has black spots, but only the upper quarter of its tail and the lower half of its dorsal fin are spotted. Another identifying factor is that its mouth is black but not its gums.

ADDITIONAL INFORMATION: Cohos spawn between mid-September and mid-November. While they generally only grow about a third the size of kings, their sizzling runs, spectacular leaps and incredible stamina endear them to legions of anglers. For some strange reason, Lake Ontario's cohos grow larger than those in the Pacific Ocean and 25-pounders are caught in the Salmon River each year. They spawn once, in the autumn of their third year, and die. The state record—and the International Game Fish Association's all-tackle world record—was caught in the Salmon River, September 27, 1989 and weighed 33 pounds, 4 ounces.

CHINOOK/COHO HYBRID ONCORHYNCHUS
A.K.A. KING-HO (*Oncorhynchus tshawytscha x kisutch*)

GENERAL DESCRIPTION: Looks like a coho—a really big one.

ADDITIONAL INFORMATION: According to Scott Prindle, "These show up from time to time." It's commonly believed they are created in the hatchery by someone mixing the wrong milt and eggs. The only way to identify this species accurately is to inspect its innards; call the NYSDEC Region 7 office in Cortland (607-753-3095) for more information.

SMALLMOUTH BASS A.K.A. BRONZEBACK (*Micropterus dolomieu*)

GENERAL DESCRIPTION: Brownish in color, it is easily differentiated from the largemouth because the ends of the mouth occur below the eyes. When hooked, its propensity for breaking water, followed through with stubborn, bulldog-like resistance earn it a lofty spot on the list of America's favorite game fish. It is granted equal status with bucketmouths in most bass tournaments. This is one of two species the DEC lists under the heading of black bass.

ADDITIONAL INFORMATION: Bronzebacks spawn in late spring and early summer when water temperatures range from 61–65 degrees Fahrenheit. The state record, caught in Lake Erie on June 4, 1995, weighed 8 pounds 4 ounces.

LARGEMOUTH BASS A.K.A. BUCKETMOUTH (*Micropterus salmoides*)

GENERAL DESCRIPTION: The largest member of the sunfish family, this species is dark green on the back and the color lightens as it approaches the white belly. A horizontal row of large, black splotches runs along the middle of the side, from the gill plate to the base of the tail. Its trademark is its huge head and mouth. The ends of the mouth reach past the eyes. This is one of two species the DEC lists under the heading of black bass in the state fishing regulations guide, and is granted equal weight with smallmouths in bass tournaments.

ADDITIONAL INFORMATION: Occurring in the entire Lower 48 states, inclined to hit artificial lures of every description, the largemouth bass is America's favorite gamefish. It'll hit just about anything that moves and is notorious for its explosive, heart-stopping strikes on surface lures. This species spawns in the spring when water temperature ranges from 62 to 65 degrees Fahrenheit. The state record, caught in Buckhorn Lake on September 11, 1987, is 11 pounds, 4 ounces.

NORTHERN PIKE A.K.A. PIKEASAURUS (*Esox lucius*)

GENERAL DESCRIPTION: The medium-sized member of the pike family, this long, slender fish is named after a spear used in combat during the Middle Ages. Its body is the same as a muskie's but its color is almost invariably green and it has large, oblong white spots on its sides. Its cheeks are fully scaled but only the top half of its gill plates are. Its teeth are razor sharp.

ADDITIONAL INFORMATION: The state record, caught in Great Sacandaga Lake on September 15, 1940, is 46 pounds 2 ounces.

CAUTION: Keep fingers out of the gill rakers; they are sharp enough to shred human flesh.

WALLEYE (*Stizostedion vitreum*)

GENERAL DESCRIPTION: The largest member of the perch family, it gets its name from its large, opaque eyes. A walleye's back is dark gray to black and fades as it slips down the sides which are often streaked in gold. It has two dorsal fins; the front one's last few spines have a black blotch at their base. Its teeth are pointed and can puncture but won't slice. Nocturnal critters, walleye often enter shallow areas to feed. If the moon is out, their eyes catch and hold the beams, spawning ghost stories and extraterrestrial sightings by folks who see the eerie lights moving around in the water. .

ADDITIONAL INFORMATION: Lake Ontario fish have been known to run as far upstream as the Black Hole. Walleye are also found in the Salmon River Reservoir. They spawn in early spring when water temperature ranges from 44 to 48 degrees Fahrenheit. The state record, caught in Mystic Lake, January 20, 2009 weighed 16 pounds 9 ounces.

YELLOW PERCH (*Perca flavescens*)

GENERAL DESCRIPTION: This popular panfish has a dark back which fades to golden-yellow sides overlaid with five to eight dark, vertical bands. Sometimes its lower fins are traced in bright orange.

ADDITIONAL INFORMATION: Partial to the slow waters of the reservoirs and river's mouth, it spawns from mid-April through May when water temperatures range from 44–54 degrees Fahrenheit. The state record, caught in Lake Erie on April 28, 1982, is 3 pounds 8 ounces.

BLACK CRAPPIE A.K.A. CALICO AND STRAWBERRY BASS (*Pomoxis nigromaculatus*)

GENERAL DESCRIPTION: Arguably the most delicious of the state's panfish, this member of the sunfish family has a dark olive or black back and silver sides streaked with gold and overlaid with black spots and blotches. The front of its dorsal fin has seven or eight sharp spines followed by a soft fan.

ADDITIONAL INFORMATION: Mostly found in the Salmon River Reservoir and Estuary, crappie spawn in late spring when water temperatures range from 57 to 73 degrees Fahrenheit. The state record, caught in Duck Lake on April 17, 1998, weighed 3 pounds, 12 ounces.

BLUEGILL (*Lepomis macrochirus*)

GENERAL DESCRIPTION: One of the most popular sunfishes, its color varies. It has anywhere from five to eight vertical bars running down the sides, a deep orange breast and a dark blue, rounded gill flap.

ADDITIONAL INFORMATION: Ounce for ounce, the bluegill is the sportiest fish. Fly fishing for them with wet flies and poppers is very popular. The species spawns in shallow, muddy areas near vegetation in summer. The state record, caught in Kohlbach Pond on August 3, 1992, is 2½ pounds.

PUMPKINSEED (*Lepomis gibbosus*)

GENERAL DESCRIPTION: This popular sunfish is the most widespread in the state. Its color ranges from bronze to dark green and its gill flap has an orange/red spot on its end.

ADDITIONAL INFORMATION: Partial to the reservoirs and slow moving water of the Estuary, the pumpkinseed spawns in shallow, muddy areas near vegetation in early summer. The state record, caught in Indian Lake on July 19, is 1 pound, 9 ounces.

ROCK BASS A.K.A. REDEYES AND GOOGLEYES (*Ambloplites rupestris*)

GENERAL DESCRIPTION: Another member of the sunfish family, it is dark brown to deep bronze in color, heavily spotted in black, and has big, red eyes.

ADDITIONAL INFORMATION: This popular panfish occupies the rocky, shallow areas of the reservoirs and lower river. The state record, caught in the Ramapo River on May 26, 1984, is 1 pound, 15 ounces.

CHANNEL CATFISH (*Ictalurus punctatus*)

GENERAL DESCRIPTION: The state's largest, indigenous member of the catfish family, it has a dark brown back, white belly, a forked tail and barbels around its mouth. Juveniles up to 24 inches have black spots on their sides. Spines on the dorsal and pectoral fins can inflict a nasty wound.

ADDITIONAL INFORMATION: Spawning takes place in summer, when water temperature reaches between 75–85 degrees Fahrenheit. The state record, caught in Lake Lauderdale on July 15, 2001, is 30 pounds.

BROWN BULLHEAD (*Ameiurus nebulosus*)

GENERAL DESCRIPTION: Having a dark brown back and white belly, this small member of the catfish family has barbels around its mouth. A relatively square tail distinguishes it from the channel catfish.

ADDITIONAL INFORMATION: Enjoying a great variety of habitats, its tolerance for high temperatures and low oxygen levels allows it to live in places other fish can't. It is found in virtually every type of water, from the Great Lakes and Adirondack ponds to the old Erie Canal. Bullhead spawn in muddy shallows late June through July. Both parents guard the schooling fry for the first few weeks of life.

The state record, caught in Sugarloaf Pond on April 26, 1998, is 6 pounds, 9 ounces.

COMMON CARP (*Cyprinus carpio*)

GENERAL DESCRIPTION: A brown colored, large-scaled fish with orange fins, it has barbels on each side of its big, round lips. Some are leather-like with no scales or spotted with disproportionately large scales

ADDITIONAL INFORMATION: Native to Eurasia, the species is one of the largest members of the minnow family, easily growing to over 30 pounds. According to some accounts, Ulysses S. Grant encouraged its introduction into the U.S. to provide American anglers with a hardy, fast growing sports fish at a time when populations of America's indigenous game species were in decline. Finding the New World good, carp thrived and spread, settling into waters from the Great Lakes and major rivers to creeks, babbling brooks, abandoned canals, drainage ditches, duck ponds, you name it. And while the species has long suffered from an image problem in this country, visiting anglers from Europe and Asia are giving it cult-like status. Its habit of foraging close to shore, combined with its propensity for exuberantly jumping clear out of the water—for no apparent reason—endear the behemoths to surprised onlookers. Carp spawn in late spring when water temperature reaches 62 degrees Fahrenheit. The state record, caught in Tomhannock Reservoir on May 12, 1995, is 50 pounds 4 ounces.

AMERICAN EEL (*Anguilla rostrata*)

GENERAL DESCRIPTION: A snakelike fish with a pointed head, its dorsal fin starts midway down its back, wraps around the end, becomes continuous with the caudal and anal fins, and reaches halfway up the belly.

ADDITIONAL INFORMATION: Born in the Atlantic Ocean, the larvae migrate to fresh water where individuals live for varying lengths of time until maturing and returning to the Sargasso Sea in autumn to spawn and die, a life cycle known as catadromous. Eels were so plentiful in the Estuary until the mid-1960s, anglers fishing for bullheads after dark caught them regularly. The state record, caught in Cayuga Lake on July 25, 1984, is 7 pounds 14 ounces.

BOWFIN A.K.A. DOG FISH (*Amia calva*)

GENERAL DESCRIPTION: Easily recognized by its primitive appearance, it has a long, flat head, a large mouth full of sharp teeth, a dorsal fin running along most of its back, and a rounded tail. Males have a large spot in the upper corner of the base of the tail.

ADDITIONAL INFORMATION: The sole surviving member of the *Amiiformes* family, a species that was around when dinosaurs roamed the countryside, bowfin spawn in shallow water in the spring. The state record, caught in Lake Champlain on July 8, 2006, is 12 pounds, 14 ounces.

WHITE SUCKER A.K.A. FRENCH TROUT AND RUBBER LIPS (*Catostomus commersoni*)

GENERAL DESCRIPTION: A large-scaled, cylindrically-shaped fish, its back and sides are olive-brown and it has a white belly. They normally range from 10 to 20 inches.

ADDITIONAL INFORMATION: Although their flesh is sweet in the early spring, it gets funky as the water warms up. Many anglers kill them needlessly and this is a waste because suckers are valuable forage for everything from pike and bass to muskies, walleyes and trout. The state record, caught in the Hudson River on May 13, 1994, is 5 pounds, 3 ounces.

RAINBOW SMELT (*Osmerus mordax*)

GENERAL DESCRIPTION: A cylindrically-shaped silver fish with an olive back, it generally sports a noticeable silver stripe and a pink or blue iridescence along it sides. It has a large mouth for a small fish with two large canine teeth on the roof. Normally ranging from six to nine inches, they can reach 13 inches.

ADDITIONAL INFORMATION: Smelt are considered a delicacy wherever they are found. They ascend streams in the spring to spawn and are often taken with dip nets. There is no state record.

LONGNOSE GAR OR GAR PIKE (*Lepisosteus osseus*)

GENERAL DESCRIPTION: Its long, narrow snout makes this fish easily identifiable. Spotted, brown or olive in color, it is often called gar pike because of its pike-like appearance: toothy snout (up to twice as long as its head) and short dorsal fin located far on its back, almost at the tail. Its flesh is edible but tastes too funky for most palates; its roe is toxic.

ADDITIONAL INFORMATION: Gars have been around for about 100 million years, and its appearance hasn't changed since the days of the dinosaurs. They can tolerate waters with low oxygen levels because their swim bladder allows them to breathe air. The state record, caught in Lake Champlain, is 13 pounds, 3 ounces.

FALLFISH (*Semotilus corporalis*)

GENERAL DESCRIPTION: Fairly long, big-eyed and plated with large silvery scales, this member of the chub family typically runs six to 18 inches and is the largest minnow native to Eastern North America.

ADDITIONAL INFORMATION: Tasting as fishy as they smell, fallfish are notorious for their savage strikes and spirited fight. They'll hit just about anything from worms and minnows to lures and flies. While they've disappointed a lot of anglers who thought they had a respectable trout on the line, they've also saved a lot of fly-fishing trips when the trout weren't biting.

ROUND GOBY (*Neogobius melanostomus*)

GENERAL DESCRIPTION: Typically measuring less than six inches long, gray and mottled with dark spots, this slope-headed, bottom dweller has big frog-like eyes high atop its head, a large black spot at the rear of its first dorsal fin and a single, fan-shaped pelvic fin.

ADDITIONAL INFORMATION: First discovered in America in the St. Clare River in 1990, these natives of Eastern Europe have spread throughout the Great Lakes watershed. Highly aggressive, feeding on just about anything live that fits in their mouths, they are especially fond of zebra mussels, worms, fish eggs and fry. Prolific breeders, they reproduce multiple times each year, providing a constant supply of bite-sized minnows for every piscivorous species in the drink, from yellow perch and crappies to landlocked Atlantic salmon and black bass. There is no state record.

Holey Fish

Up until the early years of the 19th century, the tiniest Great Lake was ruled by landlocked Atlantic salmon. Every tributary worth its weight in water hosted spawning runs from late summer through autumn. The lower Salmon River, from its 110-foot-high falls to the mouth, a distance of roughly 20 miles, drew more landlocks than any other Lake Ontario tributary.

According to Wikipedia, they ran the river in such great numbers, the hamlet of Pulaski was variously called "Fishville" and "Salmon River" before it was incorporated in 1832. Local farmers drove teams into the rapids and speared wagonloads with pitchforks; housewives waded in and caught dinner in their aprons; schoolboys clubbed them with baseball bats.

A combination of overfishing, pollution, deforestation, dams blocking natal streams, and sea lampreys invading via the Erie and Oswego Canals posed insurmountable challenges, sending Lake Ontrio's salmon over the brink by the end of the 19th century. Several attempts to stock chinooks and reintroduce Atlantic salmon into the system between 1873 and 1898, and between 1939 and 1959, met with failure.

Lake Ontario never totally gave up on her salmonids, however. "From the '40s to the '60s, anglers from all over came up to the Salmon River to fish for lake-run rainbows," claims Eddie Stempian of Syracuse. "Worms work great after a rain."

"But the fishing wasn't always rosy," he recalls. "In some cases, it was heartbreaking and disgusting."

"Lampreys were the problem," Stempian explains. "The bigger the fish, the more likely it was to have one sometimes two, vampire holes the size of quarters. Catching a once-in-a-lifetime rainbow that looked like it got shot once or twice with a deer slug turned a lot of guys off."

"Even worse was catching a fish with a lamprey still attached to it," remembers the retired painter, a shudder running through him. "Most let go while you were lifting the fish out of the water, leaving you with a holey fish . . . a hole in your soul," revealed Stempian, poetically.

"As disturbing as the sight of one was, though, it was nothing compared to having to handle it. Every now and then you'd catch a rainbow with a lamprey attached so stubbornly, you'd have to literally pull the thing off the fish . . . unless you cut the head off . . . but then you still had to get the head off the trout. And that was disturbing," admitted Stempian with disgust.

"You'd grab the slippery thing and pull. It seemed to stretch forever and ever. Slime dripped off your fingers. If you got some on your pants, you'd have to wash it off right away or face people looking at you like you were a perv. . . . The problem got so bad, most of my fishing buddies stopped coming up," revealed Stempian.

Anglers weren't the only ones who had nightmarish encounters with the blood suckers on the river back then. About as squeamish as they come, Cousin Staash recalls—over and over—his first experience with the parasites.

"It's a nightmare I can't shake," he explains. "It happened late in the summer of 1971. I remember the year because I was discharged from the Army that February. There I was, sitting on a huge rock at the edge of the Black Hole, tapping my feet on the ground to the beat of 'In A Gadda DaVida,' playing on the radio. Something squirming in the sand off to my left catches my eye. I look over . . . To my horror, several eight- to 12-inch lampreys are crawling out of the sand like in a monster movie. I didn't know if they're emerging because they're mesmerized by the song, because they can't stand the vibrations my feet were making, or if they were coming after me . . . They just kept coming out of the sand . . . Dozens of 'em! I haven't gone into the river barefoot or in shorts since," claims Staash, a look of horror sweeping over his face.

The lamprey infestation results in a steady stream of complaints to authorities. Everyone from local bait shop owners and restaurateurs to animal rights activists go into action, swamping the offices of their representatives with letters demanding immediate remediation.

Equally important, the NYSDEC had a new hatchery on the drawing board for Altmar. If something wasn't done soon, the facility faced becoming a food processing plant for the parasites.

The state finally gets off the pot at the end of the 60s, begins poisoning the things and blocking their way to the spawning grounds. By 1972, the NYSDEC's efforts to eradicate lampreys proved hugely successful, paving the way for the salmon stocking program.

"It worked!" confirms Stempian warmly, a beaming smile tightening his wrinkles. "By the end of the 70s, fish with holes in them were the exception, not the rule."

Kids Play

Teaching a kid how to fish poses two main challenges: making the lessons interesting and keeping your cool.

That's easy on the lower Salmon River

Famous for breaking local and world records, mere mention of the stream sends waves of excitement running through a child. Flowing wide under a largely open sky, casting is easy, even for the clumsiest youngster. Lastly, the sight of the large migratory species running rapids, aging anglers in hot pursuit, is an entertaining experience impossible to forget.

However, it's fraught with dangers as well. River-wide rapids, an unusually slippery floor, and regular (almost daily) water releases by the power plant at Bennetts Bridge are enough to ruin the best laid plans.

Fortunately, common sense protects us from these dangers. All you have to do is let a kid know about them, and you'll be surprised how attentive a child becomes to his surroundings.

Salmon River Fish Hatchery

Built in 1995, fed by springs that feed Beaver Dam Brook, a tributary of the Salmon River in Altmar, NY, the Salmon River Fish Hatchery enjoys a reputation as one of the finest fish-rearing facilities in the world. Producing more than 3,000,000 salmonids annually, it is the major source of trout and salmon for Lakes Erie and Ontario.

Fish that make it to the hatchery are the lucky ones, relatively speaking. The roughly 15-mile (the distance depends on how many turns the fish takes, says NYSDEC aquatic biologist Ian Blackburn) swim upriver is fraught with dangers ranging from anglers and rocky rapids to wildly fluctuating water levels.

Those that complete the trip are placed into tanks filled with water to which a sedative has been added. When the time is right, facility employees club them to knock them out. Females are sliced open, their eggs removed and placed in deep-sided plastic trays. Males are held over the eggs and squeezed, releasing a stream of milt. Hatchery employees mix the stuff and place it into containers fed fresh springwater by hoses attached to the top.

When the facility's needs are met, the door is shut. But the fish keep coming. Filled with milt and eggs, they desperately search for a way to get around the barrier blocking them from swimming up Beaverdam Brook. Hooked by the scent of their natal stream, most mill around its narrow confines. Growing increasingly desperate with each passing hour, reaching the point where they can't hold it anymore, they spawn where they are.

Some, however, break the rules and head back to the river, spawning in any tributary they can find: Orwell and Trout Brooks, unnamed springs, even, according to cousin Staash, storm run-off.

Freed of the need to spawn, their lives finally slow down. Hunger isn't an issue now, and autumn nights cool the water to comfortable levels. Exhausted, with no particular place to go, they just mill around in pools and runs . . . and wait.

Most die quickly. Others swim aimlessly in the river, rotting along the way.

Indeed, life clings so tenaciously to some salmon, they spend their last hours rubbing holes into their empty bellies and wearing away the bottoms of their tails on the shallow river's floor. Some even start dropping chunks of rotting flesh.

By late October, the run is all but over. The majority of the salmon have spawned and died; their bodies swept onshore or back into the lake to the delight of scavengers.

However, late bloomers, those that nature spares a while longer to insure the survival of the species in the event a natural catastrophe like an earthquake or volcanic eruption (common events in their home range) destroys the main run, trickle to the hatchery well into November; a few lonely individuals even come as late as December.

Salmon River International Sport Fishing Museum

New York boasts two of the world's finest fishing museums, both located on world famous trout streams. Oswego County's Salmon River International Sport Fishing Museum is the most complete.

Truth be told, the Catskill Fly Fishing Center and museum in Livingston Manor, on the banks of Willowemoc Creek, a tributary of the Beaver Kill River, which flows into the East Branch of the Delaware River, is more famous. That's mostly because it's been around for about 20 years longer, is located in the Catskills, the cradle of American fly-fishing, and is only about 50 miles from New York City.

But the Salmon River is rapidly becoming the top dog—it's already the most famous in the Lower 48 states. Another, equally important factor that'll propel the SRISFM into the front of the pack is its inclusiveness; it covers all aspects of fishing, from casting and spinning reels to trolling rods, eel spears, lures and trout creels.

But there's more to the place than fishing equipment. The walls are plastered with fine art. Everything is represented, from fanciful Romantic era fishing scenes to realistic oils by masters like Maynard Reese.

Run by volunteers, the hours aren't set in stone. However, the lobby offers loads of literature and is always open.

The museum is located at 3044 State Route 13, 2.3 miles east of CR 2A. For more information, call 315-298-2213, visit www.salmonriver internationalsportfishingmuseum.org. or the Museum's Facebook page.

PART II

FEEDER STREAMS AND NEARBY WATERS

Mad River

Sired by the union of its North and South branches in the Lewis County Town of Montague, this river pours through the wilds of the Tug Hill Plateau, drinking tributaries, including the Beaver River in the town of Redfield, before feeding the North Branch of the Salmon River off Harvester Mill Road. The state offers 6.6 miles of fishing access on its lower reaches, its most productive area, from just east of the Lewis County line all the way to its mouth on the North Branch of the Salmon River, a couple of miles north of the hamlet of Redfield. Parking and access are available off Otto Mills Drive (you'll have to hike in about a half mile).

This stream is stocked with about 320 brook trout measuring from 8 to 9 inches annually. Locals catch most of them by the end of May

Fishing is easiest in the spring before the banks get overgrown. Worms work best in the spring, and after summer and early autumn rains. Salted minnows, wet flies, flat wing streamers and wooly buggers work any time. Nymphs and dry flies are productive from late May to the end of trout season.

Mill Stream

Springing out of the wilds in the southwestern corner of Lewis County, this stream doesn't even see a road until it goes under CR 47, just east of its intersection with Harvester Mill Road.

Small, lined with heavy brush, difficult to access, this stream doesn't get stocked by the state. Still, it boasts 6.3 miles of public fishing access (0.5 miles downstream and 5.8 miles upstream of CR 47), and its colorful native brook trout make the effort of fishing it worthwhile. It's easiest to fish in the spring before the brush lining the banks gets too thick.

A convenient way to fish this creek is to park in the North Branch Salmon River Public Access lot on CR 47, a little south of its intersection with Harvester Mill Road, and fish downstream for a few hundred feet. The mouth of Mill Stream will be on the left.

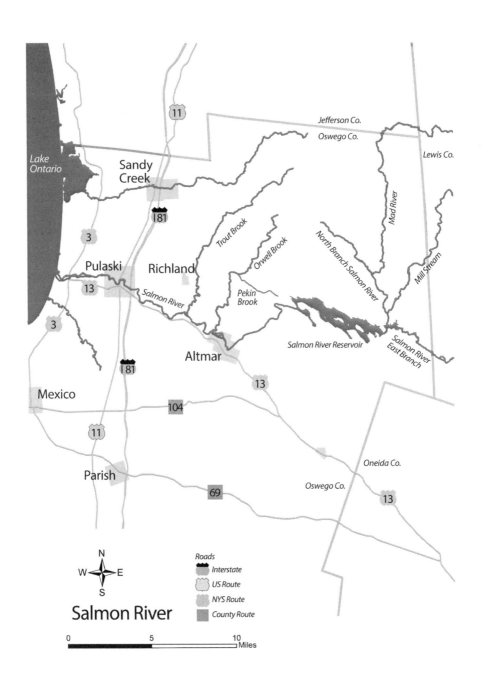

Salmon River feeder streams and tributaries.

North Branch

Tracing its roots to the convergence of numerous streams in the north-western corner of the town of Redfield, the North Branch of the Salmon River tumbles south along County Route 17 for a dozen miles or so, growing to creek-size by the time it feeds the East Branch in the hamlet of Redfield. The state negotiated 8.9 miles of PFR on the stream, and an additional 6.6 miles of PFR on its largest tributary, the Mad River. Fishing these cold, narrow, squeaky-clean headwaters is challenging but their colorful natives will have you coming back for more.

The state takes some of the pressure off the natives by stocking about 3,000 hatchery-bred brookies averaging nine inches annually. Cooped-up in concrete runways for most of their lives, the stockies' colors are as dull as cement. However, it only takes a few weeks for the cold, pristine stream to dress them in the brilliant hues their species is known for.

Public fishing access and parking are available at the CR 47 bridge on the hamlet of Redfield's east side, and on Harvester Mill Road (it heads north just past the above site) about two miles north of its inter-section with CR 47.

Salmon River (East Branch)

You know a body of water has gotta be productive if it's named after one of the world's most popular gamefish. While the lower stretch open to fishing below the Lighthouse Hill Reservoir (fishing isn't allowed for 0.5 miles below the dam) lives up to its international image as one of the country's most productive salmonid fisheries, the impoundment's dam blocks Lake Ontario's fish from going any further.

Still, the upper river's good trout bite, wrapped in marvelous scenery steeped in precious solitude, makes casting a line up here always worthwhile. Spawned by the union of its East and West Forks about a Spey cast's distance upstream of the CR 46 Bridge, some four miles east of the Lewis County hamlet of Osceola, the upper river is only about the size of a large creek when it pours into its namesake reservoir in the hamlet of Redfield.

Brookies and rainbows rule up here. Only averaging about five inches long, there's a lot of 'em and they're always hungry. And while trout this size are nothing to brag about, "there is some carry-over," claims state fisheries biologist Scott Prindle, "and fish running from six to 10 inches are fairly common."

"Fishing for trout in the river above the upper reservoir has always been challenging," adds Prindle, explaining: "The stream flows over a lot of bedrock . . . there aren't enough nutrients to support a thriving food source . . . survival is especially hard in winter . . . bass from the reservoir are moving up into the branches and tributaries . . ."

It's unlikely bass will have much effect on trout up here, however. Streamlined, boasting a taste for aquatic fare like insects, minnows and fish eggs, and terrestrial goodies like worms and grubs swept in by run-off, trout are made for shallow rapids slicing through hardscrabble habitats in deep woods. Bass . . . not so much.

Oh, they're up here all right, but they're generally small. You see, the upper river's forks (north and east branches) and tributaries are fast, shallow, narrow and cold—decent salmonid territory but not very appealing to bass. They prefer the safety, relatively warm temperatures and convenience of the reservoir's expansive, food-rich waters. Mature bass that remain in the upper river after spawning usually hang out in the pool on the east side of CR 17, seldom venturing more than a few swipes of the tail upstream beyond sight of the bridge.

Salmon River Reservoir

Fed by the East Branch Salmon River, the North Branch Salmon River, and numerous brooks and springs, this 2,660-acre impoundment is held back by a dam constructed in 1912, about five miles west of the hamlet of Redfield. Also called Redfield Reservoir, it's the largest of the stream's two impoundments. Its claim to fame is bass; largemouths outnumber smallmouths two to one.

Built to generate power (curiously, there's no hydroelectric facility anywhere near the place; a pipe at the dam carries the water a couple of miles downhill to the power plant at Bennett Bridges, at the head of the lower reservoir), the impoundment's water level fluctuates constantly, and is the main reason the reservoir is poor in aquatic vegetation. Indeed, the water level can change so much overnight, the flats you fished just before dark may be too shallow to hold fish in the morning.

Usually the change in water level isn't that drastic. Most bass just suck it up and go with the flow. Many find comfort in the caressing currents at the mouths of tributaries. The reservoir's largest, the Salmon River, draws the majority.

All the impoundment's bass run the river at one time or other, for reasons ranging from searching for new digs, food and spawning grounds, to simply wanting to see what they can see. Most find the narrow confines and shallow rapids uncomfortable to downright dangerous, and quickly beat fins back to the reservoir. On the way, some settle into habitats near the mouth; the drop-off paralleling the eastern shoulder of CR 17 in Redfield, for instance.

The vast majority, however, heads for the safety of the main reservoir (the channel just downstream of the CR 17 bridge is a popular first stop).

Relatively poor in rooted vegetation, the reservoir is loaded with other types of dynamite bass habitat. Riprap, sunken timber, stump-studded flats, boulder fields and tributary mouths skirt the place, while its open water is punctuated with shoals and islands. The south shore is so bass-friendly, in fact, an ambitious hawg with a serious case of wanderlust would be hard pressed to cover it all in a lifetime.

Spring and fall draw bass toward shore, into habitat that is productive and risky. Squeaky-clean, barely covering their backs, the clear water makes them nervous, but its ample food supply is hard to resist. Driven by their stomachs, tempered by instinct, they climb into the shallows cautiously, eyes wide open, lateral lines (running along the sides, from head to tail, they detect vibrations) at peak sensitivity.

As hazardous as this behavior is, bass have been doing it for as long as they can remember, getting pretty good at it. The slightest thing out of the ordinary—your shadow fanning the area, the sound of something dropping in the boat—sends them beating fins for cover.

While angling from a boat in shallow water has its challenges— being spotted by the fish is a big one—they're easily surmountable. Fish are used to floating objects like logs, boats, and shadows of clouds. Their flight or fight instincts are triggered by surprises, like sudden noises made by careless anglers dropping things in the boat or banging its sides. You can prevent sounding alarms by moving slowly and quietly, wearing soft-soled footgear like sneakers, holding on to gear so it doesn't drop, and casting away from your shadow.

Vibrations are a different matter. Produced by everything from movements on shore to fleeing preyfish, they're picked up by lateral lines. Running from head to tail on both sides, the system alerts fish of danger and enables them to locate prey, particularly in muddy water. Lateral lines never lie: studies show trout can differentiate between a cow and man from the vibration of their feet hitting the ground.

The heat of summer sends bass hovering over deep weeds—15 feet down or better—during daylight. They don't need sprawling weed beds down there, just enough to offer a little cover. Indeed, if you see a weed top in deep water, there's a good chance there's more below it; and a bass or two. Cast a jig—plain or tipped with bait or a trailer—right into it to find out.

All the popular bass techniques produce: bucktail jigs fished plain or tipped with bait or finesse worms and worked along channel drops; Carolina- and Texas-rigged worms dragged slowly on bottom in five to 20 feet of water (start shallow in May and go deeper as the weather gets warmer, reversing the process in autumn); poppers and darters worked over flats; jig 'n pigs fished in stump fields; weightless, wacky-rigged rubber worms tossed into timber and over rock piles, minnowbaits jerked along channel drops . . . and, of course, drifting live bait.

Aggressive, territorial, blessed with some of the biggest mouths in the water, bass are more likely than most fish to swallow live bait; and that seldom ends well for them. That's the main reason state law prohibits fishing for them with live bait (even catch and release) when their season is closed, December 1 through the Friday preceding the first Saturday in June.

Human intervention into the reservoir's fishery can be traced back to the 1930s, when the place was stocked with brown, brook and rainbow trout. Browns and rainbows are still stocked periodically, and native brookies move in when they get too big for their home streams, drawing a decent following who generally targets them by trolling minnowbaits and spoons.

Browns and rainbows, along with a few brookies, move in and out of the reservoir constantly. They're especially drawn to the ancient river channel on both sides of the CR 17 bridge, autumn through late spring. What's more, they cruise the impoundment's shoreline—the closer to tributaries the better—in five to 15 feet of water from mid-fall through spring. Come summer, they move into deep water.

One of Oswego County's greatest fishing secrets is the reservoir's walleyes. In 2004, DEC implemented a program, stocking "up to 64,000 pond fingerling walleye (1.5 to 2.5 inches) . . . for five consecutive years . . ." Finding the place to their liking, they moved right in, and typically range from too short to 21 inches long—larger ones are relatively common.

Curiously, according to state fisheries biologist Dave Lemon, the program didn't appear to be working in its early years so it was discontinued. "It was reinstated however, when locals started catching walleye regularly and began talking about it with the department," claims Lemon.

In spring and autumn, walleye spend their days on bottom—or close to it—along drop offs, in 10 to 20 feet of water, and respond to drifted nightcrawlers, bucktail jigs fished straight or tipped with scented plastics like Berkley Power Grubs, and crankbaits like Storm's Deep Thundersticks. They're also suckers for harness-rigged nightcrawlers drifted just off the floor.

An hour before dusk to an hour after dawn, walleye come close to shore, particularly around the mouths of tributaries. They'll hit black/chrome crankbaits and silver spoons in water as shallow as three feet deep.

Come summer, "eyes" spend daytime deep, responding to worms and minnows drifted just off bottom, and jigs bounced off the floor in water 15 to 40 feet deep. An hour before dusk to shortly after dawn, they move in close to shore (the later the hour, the closer they come) and hit artificials like Storm's ThunderSticks and Bass Pro Shops' Extreme Minnows worked at a moderate clip in three to 15 feet of water.

Winter sees walleyes hanging out in the same depths as summer. They respond to minnows fished plain, tipping to ice jigs tipped with minnows or insect larvae, and tiny lures like Swedish Pimples jigged deep on bottom and minnows fished plain below tip-ups.

Walleye availability varies greatly from year to year. Most blame the inconsistency on fluctuating water levels caused by draw-downs for energy production and to keep the lower river's base flow at levels mandated by the state.

At press time, walleye enjoy special protection: the minimum length is 18 inches and the daily limit is three.

Crappie are one of the reservoir's most popular items. Typically running from nine to 12 inches, autumn and spring find them around the CR 17 bridge, along the edges of the pool on the east side of the highway, and on rocky drop-offs in five to 15 feet of water, especially near the dam. In summer, they're drawn to tree branches scratching the surface, and floating or submerged timber reaching out from the bank.

These delicious beasties are suckers for minnows, in-line spinners, bucktail and maribou jigs, tiny spoons, poppers, 2- and 3-inch Power Grubs—and just about anything else that moves and fits in their mouths—and they have relatively big yaps.

One species that thrives in a rocky, vegetation-challenged reservoir like this is rock bass; typically running about half-a-pound, rockies twice that size are possible. Blessed with the biggest mouths in panfishdom, with appetites to match, they'll hit worms, crayfish, minnows, flies, poppers, anything bite-sized that moves.

Pumpkinseeds and yellow perch are numerous. The cool, squeaky-clean, water makes them exceptionally tasty. Drift for these spunky beasties with worms on bottom or suspended below floats.

An especially thrilling way to catch a mixed batch of panfish and crappies is with dry flies and poppers on a 4 or 5wt. fly-fishing outfit. Just about any fly will catch their attention.

Access to the reservoir is plentiful—and free.

Falls Road Day Use Project offers a beach launch suitable for small trailered craft, parking for about 20 rigs and shore fishing access. Head east out of Pulaski on CR 2 for about nine miles, turn right on Dam Road, travel for 1.2 miles and turn left at the four corners. Dam Road isn't plowed in winter.

Jackson Road Public Access has a double wide concrete launch, parking for 40 rigs and shore fishing access. Head east out of Pulaski on CR 2 for about 9.5 miles and turn right on Jackson Road (the lower half of Jackson Road isn't plowed in winter).

Little America Public Access boasts a beach launch, parking for about thirty rigs, and shore fishing access. Take CR 2 east out of Pulaski for just under 11 miles, turn right on C.C.C. Drive, and travel for about 0.5 mile. The lower portion of C.C.C. Drive isn't plowed in winter. This site's steep banks make launching even small canoes difficult. There are several hardened, no-frills campsites above the east side of the parking lot and one on the road leading to the access site.

In the hamlet of Redfield, County Route 17 offers two public access sites with hard surface launches and parking: one on the northeastern corner of the reservoir, the other a few hundred yards further down the road, at the bridge, where CR 17 turns west (across from Waterbury Road) and follows the lake for a short distance.

Hall Island State Forest Public Access: This site has upper and lower parking lots. If the upper barrier is closed, you'll have to park and walk 0.8 mile to the reservoir. To get there, head south on NY 13 from Pulaski for about 6.5 miles to Altmar. Turn left on Cemetery Road (CR 22) at the Salmon River Fish Hatchery sign and continue for 3.2 miles. Turn south just before the bridge over the power company's discharge channel onto CR 30, travel for 0.3 mile, bear left onto Pipeline Road and travel 2.2 miles to the parking area and access road on the left. This is a popular night-bite for bullhead in spring.

Running along roughly 90 percent of the south shore, from Dam Road on the west side to CR 17 on the east end, primitive camping is allowed in Hall Island State Forest. State law requires campsites be at least 150 feet from the bank, trail or road. Camping is limited to groups of nine or less and for up to three nights. Larger groups, and stays lasting four nights or longer, require a permit from the local forest ranger (607) 753-3095 ext. 217.

Between the Reservoirs

Most of the river from the upper reservoir is piped (along Pipe Line Road, no less) to the power plant at the head of Lighthouse Hill Reservoir. A little, barely enough to fill a skinny creek, is allowed into the old riverbed between the impoundments to keep the 110-foot high Salmon River Falls running, one of Oswego County's most popular attractions.

Upstream of the cataract, the river flows shallow, over bedrock, reaching summer temperatures ideal for a variety of creek minnows, but too warm for trout.

Fishing improves dramatically downstream of the falls. Springs pouring off and seeping out of the cliffs keep the river cool. Remote, rugged, lacking a well-defined path, running over some of the flattest and slipperiest riverbed imaginable, this stretch doesn't see many anglers; but it holds some nice trout, mainly browns and rainbows, punctuated with a few native brookies. Tracing their roots to the lower reservoir, the browns and rainbows run this stretch to spawn. Many find the caressing, squeaky-clean water to their liking and stay.

The plunge pool is home to massive quantities of smallmouth bass averaging 10 inches. What they lack in size they more than make up for with violent strikes and aerial combat. While they'll hit spoons, spinners, crayfish, minnows, worms and all the other usual suspects, working streamers through the pool at a rapid clip is far more exciting and productive.

Browns can reach 20-something inches. Their numbers have been off lately because the authorities have stopped stocking them in the lower reservoir. But the fish that are available are bigger.

Wild brookies find their way into this part of the river when they outgrow their natal waters. Many find life pretty good in the plunge pool, fall through spring. In summer, however, unbearable temperatures drive most of them into spring holes.

Fallfish typically average five inches, but eight-inchers—even longer—are available.

These fish didn't survive the austere conditions on this short stretch of river by being careless, and the first sign something ain't right sends them diving for cover into rapids or cracks in the floor, where their spots and colors blend in perfectly with surface glare, bubbles and bedrock.

Salmon River Falls from the overlook on Falls Road.

Avoid drawing attention to yourself by blending in with the surroundings and staying quiet. Wear a sky-colored shirt while wading out a ways; green or brown when fishing from shore. Tread lightly and slowly, making sure you don't kick rocks, snap sticks, or step on branches poking into the water. Stay as close to the bank as you can so you blend in with the trees and cliffs.

Most important of all, stay calm when a large trout swims into view—one cast is all you'll usually get.

Boasting some big holes along a wide riverbed largely devoid of vegetation, this stretch is ideal for swinging streamers like wooly buggers and blacknosed daces through holes, or casting them upstream in the current and retrieving quickly, so they'll skim the surface like a minnow in flight.

Nymphs cast along the edges of rapids and allowed to go with the flow, or cast upstream and retrieved in time with the current so there's no drag; and dry flies cast into pools or skittered over ripples, also produce strikes.

Still, even if you spook the fish or they have lock jaw, sending you home with nothing but fishy fantasies and excuses, the gorge's visual feast and symphony of breezes, rustling leaves and rushing water make the effort of getting there worthwhile.

On a more civilized note, the water in the pool directly below the powerhouse at Bennett Bridges is loaded with trout—and easy to fish. The power company posts the short stretch of bank on both sides of the tailrace downstream to CR 22, so you'll have to fish from the bridge and pull the fish up about 12 feet. Lob a salted minnow (the force of the cast will tear a live one off the hook) or worm on a bobber as close to the powerhouse as possible and let it drift through the discharge pool.

Lighthouse Hill Reservoir (Bennett Bridges)

Spawned by the convergence of the powerhouse tailrace and what's left of the free-flowing river at Bennett Bridges, roughly two miles downstream of the Salmon River Reservoir, this impoundment traces its roots to the completion of the Lighthouse Hill dam in 1930. Tucked

Powerhouse tailrace at Bennett Bridges.

into the hills off the beaten path, averaging 25 feet deep and dropping to a maximum depth of 50 feet, this "fishin' hole" is seldom talked about.

With good reason: only covering 164 acres, it can get awfully crowded when there's more than one boat on it. The authorities help keep it off the radar by prohibiting motors, which limits angler interest to purists who get thrills out of catching bass in a beautiful spot shrouded in silence. So keeping it out of the public eye is an honored tradition around these parts.

Still, the place sees quite a few anglers (they can't keep a secret). Jim Everard, a fisheries biologist with the DEC office in Cortland, says: "We stock 4,300 rainbows between eight to nine inches into the reservoir each spring, drawing early season anglers who learn about it in the DEC's trout stocking lists" (www.dec.ny.gov/outdoor).

That's a lot of trout for a place this size. They respond to wet flies worked in the mouth of the powerhouse tailrace (especially around dawn and dusk), spoons and in-line spinners cast and trolled along the shoreline, and tiny jigs tipped with minnows and bounced on bottom along drop-offs.

Rick Smith, a local guide intimately familiar with the place, claims bucketmouths are its most popular gamefish. Typically ranging from too short to 18 inches, hawgs stretching the tape over 20 inches and weighing up to five pounds are taken regularly; six-pounders have been reported.

"This place has some nice smallies, too," adds Smith. "There aren't as many as there are largemouths, but they average two pounds, always seem to be hungry and fight hard."

Best of all, the bass are easy to locate. The place doesn't have much vegetation so they congregate around any structure they can find like submerged timber, boulder fields and drop-offs. Smith likes to drift over these areas and fly-fish with poppers.

As often as not, however, wind riles the surface too much for top-water lures. Drifting quietly and jerking stickbaits along the shoreline, running streamers with a sinking line through the tailrace and working jigs along the deep ends of drop-offs will generally fill your live-well with smallies and bucketmouths.

Black crappie, yellow perch, pumpkinseeds, bluegills, rock bass and bullheads are plentiful, too. All but the bullheads hit flies and poppers; crappies, rockies and perch can't keep their mouths shut around minnows, and all but the crappies like worms.

Most of the reservoir's shoreline is open to the public. The only exceptions are the short stretch of tailrace between the power plant and the bridge on the east end and the bank around the dam and power plant on the west end.

The Salmon River Project Bennett Bridges Day Use Site on CR 22 offers parking for about 20 cars, a beach launch (electric motors only) and several hundred yards of shore fishing access, including on the reservoir's most productive spot, the mouth of the power company's tailrace.

As any trout angler worth his weight in split-shot can tell you, trout like current. The water coming out of the Bennett Bridges powerhouse is normally 10 times the volume of the flow allowed into the natural riverbed. The reason is that the vast majority of the water coming out of the Salmon River Reservoir is piped to the power plant, leaving just enough in the old stream to feed the Salmon River Falls, a popular tourist attraction.

To get to the reservoir from Pulaski, head south on NY 13 for 6.8 miles to Altmar. Turn left on Cemetery Road (at the Salmon River Hatchery sign), and continue straight (it turns into CR 22) for 3.4 miles. A beach launch with parking for about 10 rigs is on the left, nestled between the bridges. Launch at the hard surface ramp on the tailrace. Take out on the old river, directly across from where you launched— you might have to pull the boat over a shallow spot at the mouth during low water.

Another access site is the Salmon River Project Picnic Area and Canoe Launch, offering a couple of hundred yards of bank fishing, a beach launch, parking for five cars and a picnic table.

From the site above, head north on CR 22, cross the bridge, take an immediate left onto Hog Back Road and travel a few hundred feet.

Lower Tributaries

Draining 285 square miles, the lower Salmon River didn't become famous internationally on its own. It owes a lot to its tributaries: they feed it, cool it, and provide spawning grounds for Lake Ontario's salmon and trout. Without its feeders, the stream would be just another pretty little wiggly blue line on the map.

Pekin Brook

This skinny creek draws mature salmon and steelhead from Orwell Brook.

Parking and public access to about 0.5 miles of water are available at its mouth on CR 52, a few hundred feet west of the intersection with Tubbs Road.

Orwell Brook

Feeding the river a couple of hundred yards upstream of the Trestle Pool, this skinny creek is an important spawning area for salmon, steelhead and brown trout. Its undercut banks, windfalls, pools and rapids hold salmon during the run, and trout from fall through spring. This stream doesn't get stocked.

Much of it is open to the public. The brook's lower reaches are easy to get to from the Salmon River's Trestle Pool North parking lot (its mouth is visible from here). Just walk a few hundred feet upstream on the path skirting the farmer's field to one of the steep trails leading down to the water.

Orwell Brook Fishing, a private operation, offers three miles of private fishing.

Finally, the state offers 2.9 miles of public access upstream (.75 miles) and downstream of the parking areas on Mattison and Tubbs Roads.

Trout Brook

Pouring into the Salmon River a little downstream of Pineville, this popular skinny creek is open to public fishing from NY 48 to its mouth, a little more than a half mile. Its lower reaches are punctuated with deep pools. Salmon and browns run it in autumn, steelhead are available fall through spring.

A parking area for about 25 cars is located on the right side of CR 48, about 100 yards up the road (north) from the bridge.

PART III

THE SALMON RIVER

THE FISH AND FISHING TECHNIQUES

In his "History of the Salmon River Fishery," Verdoliva writes that the current salmonid fishery traces its roots to 1968 when the NYSDEC stocked 22,000 coho salmon. Chinooks were added to the program in 1970; steelhead in 1974; and Atlantic salmon in 1996. These species have all been stocked regularly ever since.

Early on, salmonids were released directly into the river. Eggs and milt were collected from fish trapped in a weir on Spring Brook, at Maple Avenue, just east of its intersection with U.S.11, Pulaski's Main Street.

Soon after steelhead were introduced, the salmonid fishery faced the chopping block. In 1976, scientists discovered years of pollution carpeting Lake Ontario's floor in a witches' brew of dangerous chemicals like Mirex and PCBs. All the lake's critters were contaminated to some degree (the bigger the fish, the worse the corruption). Since the toxins posed a public health issue, the stocking program was put on hold; possession of salmon from the lake and its tributaries was banned; tags were made available for anglers wanting to keep fish for mounting.

Once you've tangled with Pacific salmon it's impossible to forget them. Popular opinion, combined with area merchants and local government's never ending need for revenue conspired against the ban. It was lifted a few years later. Once again, the autumn air over the lower river was filled with the whooping and hollering of excited anglers fighting salmon.

By the early '90s, it became painfully obvious that the introduction of snagging for salmon was wiping away 100 years of ethical, American fishing tradition (we're the first people in history to practice catch-and-release). Snaggers began popping up everywhere: streams in the Catskills, Adirondack ponds, lakes in municipal parks, duck ponds, public fountains, sewage treatment plants, you name it. No body of water was sacred. If it looked like it might have a fish, someone was ripping a weighted treble hook through it.

The party didn't last long. Seeing snagging as cruel and unsporting, folks ranging from ethical anglers and tree huggers to whale lovers demanded the authorities put an end to the practice.

Anti-snagging sentiment took off on a rampage. "It got so intense," says cousin Staash, "husbands turned against wives, sisters against brothers, Christians against Jews. . . . Rumor has it a couple guys got slapped around at the Sportsmens Pool just for thinking about it." (Staash's dad always said the boy's mind was like a bad sinker, a couple grams light of a full ounce.)

Responding to the spreading menace, the authorities clamped down, banning the practice of snagging Pacific salmon. By 1995, possesing "three-legged crickets" (snag hooks) on the river was forbidden. Before long, keeping foul-hooked salmonids from any of the state's waters was prohibited.

Unwilling to change their ways, unscrupulous anglers developed snagging techniques using single-pointed hooks.

The most common is lifting: raising the rod slowly while the bait swings through the current, and setting the hook at the first sign of resistance, usually foul-hooking the fish in a fin or the tail.

Coming in at a close second is flossing. Yup, it's just what it sounds like: casting the line upstream and off to the side of the fish so it goes into its mouth, and setting the hook, catching the fish in the hinge of the jaw.

Deadly when used at any level of expertise, lifting and flossing are especially devastating in the hands of skilled anglers who get away with it because they're expert rod handlers, doing it subtly, without the tell-tale "repeated or exaggerated jerking motions of the fishing rod" (DEC's definition) that gives snaggers away.

Although standard fishing gear is used to lift, the NYSDEC considers it snatching, not fishing. In the Definitions section of the "NY Freshwater Fishing" guide, the state writes: "Snatching means taking fish not attracted by bait or artificial lure with hooks, gangs or similar devises whether or not baited . . . Snagging, lifting and single-hook snagging are types of snatching."

Bad habits are hard to break, and, sure enough, snagging with weighted treble hooks still goes on. At least now, poachers only snag half the time, spending the other half looking over their shoulders to see if someone's watching.

And someone often is.

If you're gonna lift, keep in mind ECOs are savvy to all the tricks, and have a knack of showing up when least expected.

What's more, law enforcement has countless champions of the environment in its corner: hikers, photographers, Scouts, repentant ex-snatchers, ex-hippies, you name it. Armed with cell phones, fingers itching to call authorities at the first sign of a fishing violation, this hodgepodge of concientious citizens is like all volunteers: dedicated. Cousin Staash likes to say: "A cell phone in the hands of environmentalists is the greatest boon to fish and game in history."

Fortunately, most anglers are sportsmen who believe in fair chase. About the biggest challenges befuddling them are practical matters like when's the most productive time to fish.

Beyond a doubt, the best bite is at first light. And it's not because breakfast is a fish's most important meal of the day.

It's because the power company shuts down its turbines at Bennet Bridges during periods of low demand (when folks are sleeping, for instance), dropping the water level by at least half at exactly the same time that cover of darkness sparks salmon and trout out in the lake to run upstream. Since it takes about four hours for the lower water level to reach the mouth, the evening's fresh-run of salmonids are well on their way upstream by the time the water drops around them.

Even the water dropping to the point where it barely covers their backs doesn't discourage them, however. Driven by hormones instead of survival instincts, they keep pushing forward into the quiet darkness.

While ambitious fish can reach the hatchery the first night, a lot of salmon don't for a variety of reasons: Distracted by side channels and tributaries, trial and error slows a lot of them down. High water after a rain disorients quite a few, too. Some are just easygoing by nature and take their time.

Slacking has its price. Just before dawn, when angling is permitted (fishing is prohibited on the lower river from a half-hour after sunset to a half-hour before sunrise), slowpokes swim into their worst nightmare: lines of anglers straddling both sides of the misty river, whipping long rods bearing hooks.

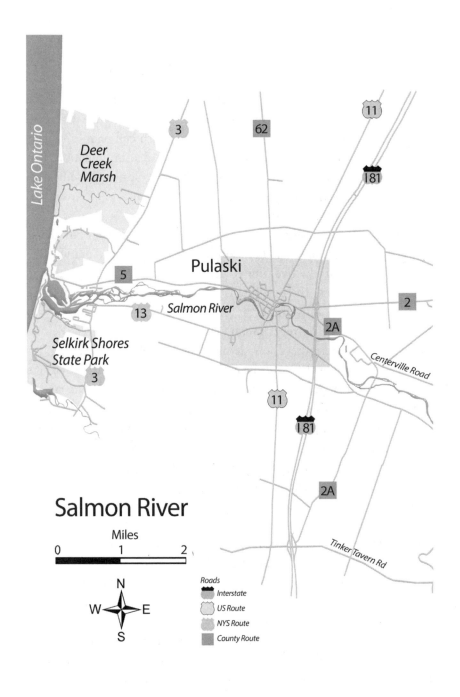

Lake Ontario

Deer
Creek
Marsh

3

62

11

I 81

5

Pulaski

13   Salmon River

2

2A

Selkirk Shores
State Park

3

11

I 81

Centerville Road

2A

Salmon River

Miles

0   1   2

Tinker Tavern Rd

N
W E
S

Roads
Interstate
US Route
NYS Route
County Route

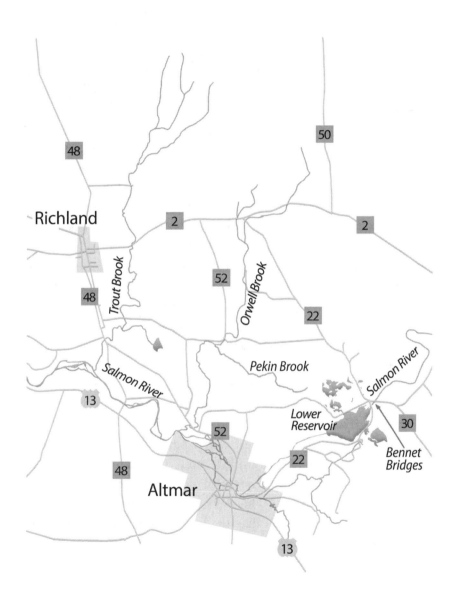

Salmon Time

Back in the early 19th century, Lake Ontario supported the greatest population of landlocked Atlantic salmon in the world. "Granted, the number of landlocks isn't anywhere near what it was in the day," says cousin Staash, "but they're commin' around. It seems more and more are caught every year. And they're getting bigger and bigger all the time."

The big pond's smelt and alewives make it so.

Don't think for a minute these little guys are a free lunch, going into that dark gullet quietly. They get even with their persecutors by waging a fishy form of chemical warfare. Their bodies are loaded with thiaminase, an enzyme that leads to a vitamin B1 (necessary for the body to turn food into energy) deficiency in Atlantic salmon and steelhead—and, to a lesser degree, Pacific salmon. Lack of the vitamin causes infertility in adults, and early mortality syndrome (Cayuga syndrome) in the offspring of the lucky few that manage to spawn successfully. Bathing the eggs in thiamine (vitamin B1), counters the enzyme's effects.

New York's native son, the Atlantic is the only salmon that survives (roughly 50%) the spawning ordeal. A small number comes back to spawn a second time, and a lucky few even get a third shot at it. Experts attribute their ability to mate multiple times—and live to talk about it—to their close kinship with brown trout.

Better known around these parts as landlocked salmon because they spend their entire lives in fresh water, they're descendants of ocean-running Atlantic salmon, the world's oldest gamefish. Roman legions fished for them on British streams with flies made of dyed mare's hair, conquering ancient England with smoked salmon on their breaths.

No one knows the exact date the first salmon will appear in the stream. A few precocious fish run in August and late bloomers sometimes wait until November; the heaviest runs generally occur from the mid-September through October.

The only way to find out if "they're really in" (one man's major run is another man's disappointing few) is to come up and see for yourself.

Atlantics are the first to show up, trickling (they don't run *en masse* like their Pacific cousins) into the river as early as May—which is surprising for a fish that doesn't spawn until late autumn. Most experts believe the fast water's high oxygen content draws them.

Prindle doesn't believe they're that practical. He thinks they run the stream in the heat of summer simply "because they can. Atlantics are the most warmwater tolerant of the species," he says, adding ". . . and they just like hanging around rapids."

They're also the most fisherman-friendly salmon, eagerly hitting worms after a rain; minnowbaits, streamers and salted minnows swung across current on sunny days; silver spoons and in-line spinners worked through pools and runs anytime, except during thunderstorms.

"They'll even take dry flies on mild summer evenings," claims Verdoliva. His favorite patterns are Royal Wulffs, Bombers, and Stimulators.

When hooked, their spirited resistance, punctuated with tall leaps and cartwheels, is legendary, endearing them to the professional and intellectual classes of anglers. In the Old Country, the Atlantic is considered king of the salmon.

Chinooks, a Pacific variety, are the world's largest salmon, and the apple in the eyes of the majority of visiting anglers that come to the river each autumn. The state ensures the economy around Pulaski keeps humming by stocking roughly 350,000 spring fingerlings into the stream each year. Prindle estimates 100,000 return to the river as mature adults.

Also called kings, chinooks live up to the image by growing anywhere from 15 to 35 pounds (they reach up to 100 pounds in their home range). While 40-pounders are out there (the state record, caught in the Salmon River in September 1991, is 47 lb., 13 oz.), fish that size mostly only swim in dreams.

Early kings enter the rapids in August. And while their numbers pale compared to the quantities that'll charge upstream next month, they're the most likely to hit a bait, and have been known to rise to a fly.

The nicest thing about these early runners is they're fresh out of the lake. Boasting dark green backs spotted in black and silvery sides, lacking the unsightly scars later fish earn fighting rapids, crowds of anglers, each other . . . and time, they make the most attractive mounts. Barely mature, they're the best tasting, too.

Cohos, another Pacific variety, share the limelight with chinooks. Roughly 90,000 fingerlings are stocked annually into Beaverdam Brook, the stream that drains the hatchery. Prindle estimates about 23,000 return as adults.

Far more manageable on light tackle, likely to make numerous leaps when hooked, and bearing silver sides with a trace of red running their entire length, cohos are considered the classier of the two and are preferred by fly-fishermen.

Pacific salmon usually run *en masse*. About five percent are immature copycats (males are called Jacks, females are called Jennies,) just following the crowd. Small groups start the ball rolling in early September. By month's end, waves, often numbering in the thousands, charge the rapids. Over the next few weeks, streams of fish, in large numbers (in 2016, it's estimated about 100,000 returned to the river, and 60,000 were caught by anglers), will buck the river daily.

The journey home is heroic. Salmon, especially kings, are so big, their bellies scratch bottom and their backs slice through the surface in wide stretches of the river. Caressing rapids that cradled them as smolts on their downstream trek to the lake three and a half years ago must be carefully scrutinized to avoid getting beached. The rocky shallows the smolts beelined through on their carefree, playful journey to the lake are so low now that the salmon have to swim sideways in spots just to get through. Boulders they used to hug for concealment from dangers like eagles and ospreys now barely cover their tails.

Their biggest surprise, however, is man. Now, instead of feeding and caring for them like we did when they were smolts, we stand in their way, water up to our privates, swinging long sticks with lines bearing hooks. Some guys even chase after them through the rapids (they've been known to wield clubs when no one's looking).

Still, they run, come men or high water; the majority between September 15 and October 15.

A few, however, always come as early as mid-August; and some wait until late October, sometimes even November. This delay in fulfilling their urges isn't by choice; it's a natural mechanism. Hailing from out West, a part of the country notorious for earthquakes and forest fires, nature staggers the run to insure there are some fish to carry the species into the future in the event a natural catastrophe wipes out the main run.

Normally, the river is simply the main route salmon take to their final destination: the tributaries. That's where the pebbles are: pebbles to make redds (hollows in the streambed where eggs are deposited) and to cover the eggs. The smaller the stream, the better the chance its floor will be covered with them.

Beds of pebbles are found in the open river, too, and salmon will spawn on them in a pinch, usually in emergencies. The main reason they don't regularly spawn in the main stream is because it's too perilous for the eggs, which are rather large compared to those of other fish species, and easily swept away by the ever-changing current. They are also easily spotted by predators, which include everything from crayfish and minnows to seagulls and trophy trout.

Seagulls (dump ducks) are the most brazen. They're known to fly over spawning salmon, swooping down to pick up eggs that are caught by the current and carried downstream.

Anglers often treat the birds to caviar inadvertently. A common sight in the village of Pulaski in autumn is that of anglers dragging salmon down the sidewalk, seagulls waddling in their footsteps, feeding on fresh eggs dropping from the fish.

Nature compensates for the dangers of the spawning grounds by allowing the fish to stop in the middle of what they're doing and flee at the first sign of trouble (often with eggs still dangling out of their bodies), and start all over again in a safer spot. Females can make as many as seven redds, depositing eggs in each.

Going after big fish in a relatively narrow, shallow stream like the Salmon River, you reap what you sow. If you're a social angler, happy to be part of the circle of guys ringing all the pools, whooping and hollering whenever somebody hooks one, any of the river's popular holes will do. All you have to do is wiggle in between the anglers, brace yourself against the current and start fishing. With all the commotion going on, the fish are spooked or angry and keep moving. Sooner or later, one'll hit your line—whether it wants to or not.

In fact, the river's largest pools host spectacles akin to the sea battles Roman emperors—Nero is the most famous—staged in the Colosseum.

But instead of miniature galleys catapulting rocks while slaves dressed as Roman soldiers board one another's ships and fight hand-to-hand combat, all to the delight of the cheering, bloodthirsty mob, the Salmon River is lined with anglers casting salmon eggs and egg-pattern flies to trophy salmonids, hooking great numbers, sending them leaping into the air to the delight of cheering crowds watching from shore and bridges (Pulaski's US 11 and downtown Altmar's CR 52 bridges are popular viewing platforms).

But there's a lot more to the salmon run than just arm-wrenching battles with trophy fish. Walking up on a couple spawning, for instance, etches a moment into your memory that's every bit as exciting as hooking a wall-hanger.

Mating couples are fairly easy to spot, too. Instead of dashing upstream with the crowd, they splash around playfully in ripples and shallow rapids; the females digging redds (nests) and depositing eggs, the males next to them, squirting milt. Excited more than they've ever been, or ever will be, they'll do the deed right in front of you, if you don't disturb them.

See for yourself. The next time you're relatively alone on the river during the salmon run (the place gets swamped with anglers in the morning, but they peter out as the day progresses) and the water is up (call Waterline to find out), walk slowly and quietly on shore along the edges of rapids. Keeping your shadow on land or behind you, search the pockets behind boulders and the edges of whitewater for patches of submerged spots that look like bubbles against dark backgrounds. Unlike bubbles, however, the spots will be stationary if the fish is resting; going against the flow if it's moving.

Experienced anglers will see the whole fish right away. If you're new to the game, however, you'll have to train your mind to look through their camouflage to see what's really there.

The first thing you're going to need is a pair of polarized sunglasses (the lenses are coated with a film that reduces glare caused by sunlight reflecting off water). Now, look out over rocky rapids (rocks provide cover, reduce the speed of the water, and create disturbances on the surface that fragment the profiles of fish). Don't concentrate on seeing a whole fish, look for parts of one. Fins or tail, for instance. If you come to what looks like an eye, concentrate on it. With a little luck, the hinge of a jaw will appear, followed, almost miraculously, by the rest of the fish.

Salmon are perfectly camouflaged in all their stages. Out in the lake, a chinook's green back and silvery sides resemble surface glare. When they mature and enter the river, the green turns brown and the sides yellow, blending in perfectly with the cliffs towering over the stream, the rocks carpeting the floor and the sun's reflection on the water.

A coho, on the other hand, is silvery in the lake. When it matures and enters the river, it sports a dark green back, with a wide, faint reddish stripe running the length of its silvery sides.

Don't go fishing in the deep part of a pool and expect salmon to hit. The fish are there all right, but they're resting or taking cover, passive behaviors that don't normally result in aggressive strikes. In fact, the fish suspend in deep pools to avoid all the hooks that are ripping across the floor.

Besides, they stop feeding upon entering the river, remember? So, your chances of a salmon chasing your bait in a pool are about as good as your chances of growing hair on a smolt.

To be successful, you've got to stop thinking too much. Leave your common sense and human values at home and act instinctively, like the fish.

For instance, their goal is to get upriver, to get it on. So it only makes sense they'll charge headlong into the rapids and keep moving. Without obstructions blocking the way, a healthy, spawn-minded salmon can make it to the hatchery's fish ladder at Beaverdam Brook in a day.

You're probably wondering: if salmon stop feeding when they enter the river, what's the sense in trying to entice them with food?

The object isn't to feed them, it's to challenge them. Biologists believe salmon strike the eggs of their own species, as well as trout eggs, to protect their own spawn from future predation and to eliminate competition their offspring will face. They attack streamers out of sheer orneriness.

Finally, it's illegal to do anything with a foul-hooked salmon except reel it in and release it immediately (remember, there's a chance you're being watched). You're not supposed to take a hero shot (photograph it), weigh it, measure it, or even kiss it (an officer of the law would probably understand, giving you a break if he sees you give it a peck on the cheek . . . but a deep kiss will land you in a heap of trouble, maybe even the mental ward).

Besides fear of the law, there's a very practical reason for releasing the fish immediately. Unlike rough, bottom feeders like catfish and carp, which can live for quite a while out of water, and can take being handled without much harm, salmon are noble critters and won't stand for much abuse. In fact, a 40-pound king will die after a few minutes out of water, roughly the same time it takes a sunfish.

While quick death may seem like Mother Nature is playing a cruel trick on them, it's actually a blessing. Pacific salmon often travel hundreds of miles to reach the spawning grounds in their native range. Besides having to deal with hungry bears along the way, they face obstacles like waterfalls, log jams and beaver dams. If they jump in the wrong spot or take the wrong channel (natural forces like high water and earthquakes constantly alter streams), they can easily get beached.

Driven by the uncontrollable urge to spawn, unable to feed, protected by laws that prohibit foul hooking them . . . what's an angler to do?

The only thing you can do—piss 'em off!

And that isn't hard to do during the run. Hormones raging, used to being the biggest kids on the block, they're cranky to begin with. All you have to do is channel that aggressive energy in your favor. The easiest place to do that is in the rapids.

Although the river's holes hold a lot of salmon, they're usually ringed with anglers by first light. The fish taking cover there get educated in the ways of hooks real quick, and avoid getting stuck by suspending.

Still, they're used to having their way. And while you'd think the river's shallow water and narrow confines would temper their aggression a bit, or at least make them a little more cautious, fighting rapids, anglers and each other all day—maybe even getting rejected by the opposite sex—gives them an attitude. It takes a lot to make them veer off course. If something smaller gets in the way, it's curtains for the hapless critter.

This is survival of the fittest in action, pure and simple: the baddest bucks get to pick the best mates; the toughest hens get the choicest spawning sites. No picking straws, affirmative action, arbitration, turning the other cheek . . . just guts and brute force.

Brown Trout

Lake browns the size of footballs run with the salmon. Not because they like them; because they spawn around the same time. Easily distinguished from Pacific salmon by their smaller size and lighter color—in the water they look pale, like ghosts, next to kings and cohos—they typically go from three to eight pounds; and specimens tipping the scales over 10 pounds are caught regularly.

There's a big difference between lake-run and river fish. Often called football browns, lake-run fish are broad, with dark brown backs, spotted in red and black, fading into gold along the sides, and white at the belly. River brown's have the same colors but they're brighter; their bodies are much more cylindrical in shape (cigar-like, explains Cousin Stash), and they're much smaller.

Native to the Old Country, browns have been dealing with man for thousands of years and aren't as impulsive or flashy as salmon or steelhead. Like most trout, their first reaction to the sting of a hook is to jump clear out of the water. If that doesn't set them free, they seldom waste valuable energy trying that again. Instead, they pull a number of tricks. Diving and taking the fight to the bottom is their favorite tactic in a pool. In rapids, they turn into the current, catch it with their side then charge, at an angle, downstream; some swim into shallow ripples on the other side and try wrapping your line around rocks or sunken timber.

Browns aren't stocked directly into the lower river. Instead, somewhere around 60,000 are released annually into Lake Ontario, off the Oswego County coast; half in the Town of Richland (the lower Salmon River runs through it) and half in the Town of Oswego, within smelling distance of the Salmon River. Bottom oriented, they like to keep their fins near the floor so they don't generally go out too far, preferring to stay in water less than 100 feet deep.

Unfortunately, their run upriver is short, over by November. The good thing is some take a liking to the rapids and settle in for the winter.

Steelhead

State fisheries biologist Scott Prindle claims the amount of time anglers spend fishing on the lower Salmon River (fishing is prohibited from a half-hour after sundown to a half hour before sunrise) in September and October equals the total angler hours spent on the rest of the stream the entire year.

That's no exaggeration. From summer's end through Halloween, the daytime population of Pulaski doubles. And noisy . . . ! Walk parallel to the river on Maple Avenue or stand on the South Jefferson Street or Salina Street bridges in the heart of Pulaski and the whoopin' and hollerin' of excited anglers, punctuated by the splashes of fish jumping, fills the air.

All that commotion doesn't just stem from roaring rapids, jumping salmon, and anglers slipping, sliding and falling in. Much of it is caused by the river's other highly prized game fish: steelhead, the ocean-running form of rainbow trout. Famed for its stubborn resistance and spectacular leaping abilities, it's one of America's most popular sport fish, drawing countless anglers from around the world to Pulaski year-round, especially in autumn.

As October drags on, sending the salmon to meet their maker, and post-spawn browns back to the big pond, steelhead pick up the slack. Originally hailing from the West Coast, they naturally run the river behind kings and cohos to dine on the caviar year-round.

The most popular steelhead bait on the river is an egg sac. Trout eggs work a little better than salmon eggs.

Single eggs are dynamite, too. Cured, natural eggs are best but they don't stay on a hook too well. Artificial eggs and ceramic beads will do, especially in fall when steelhead aren't too savvy in the ways of man . . . yet.

Chartreuse (imitating a rainbow trout minnow) or brown Wooly Buggers are the most popular streamer for chromers, especially in winter. Using a sinking line to get down deep, quickly and naturally, cast across the current and let the fly swing through it. The fish usually hits when the streamer reaches the edge of the current below you.

While there's no law against retrieving the streamer through the current or along it's edge (we all do occasionally) most guys don't feel it's productive enough to do all the time. So, at the end of the drift, they whip the rod back, sending the line behind them, then whip it forward quickly to cast out again.

If a floating line is all you have, add BB-sized split shots to the leader, 18-inches to a couple of feet above the fly. (Supplemental weight—split shots, swivels, metal leaders—are prohibited in the fly fishing section from May 1 thru August 31.) What you're looking to do is have the shot bounce on bottom while your fly bobs around just above the floor.

Scarred with fissures, carpeted with rocks, the river floor's appetite for terminal tackle is insatiable. A sinking line will get a fly deep without snagging bottom. However, if you want to work a nymph or egg pattern on the floor, you'll need some weight. You can limit the amount of tackle you lose by using a 3-way swivel, attaching split shot or pencil lead to a short leader lighter than your main line on the bottom ring. A lot of guys swear by pencil lead because it doesn't slip between the cracks as easily.

Steelies will also hit salted minnows, worms, wet flies, dry flies, glo bugs, pieces of sponge, kernel corn, you name it, at any time and in just about any weather—thunderstorms and blizzards being the only exceptions.

Finally, steelies take plugs like Kwikfish and Hotshots, and in-line spinners like Rooster Tails and Mepps Aglias. Keep them small, ⅛-ounce or less.

When hooked, their initial reaction is to take off with such power and speed, you'll think you snagged a torpedo.

A steelies' mystique is such that anglers never complain when they hook one incidentally while fishing for salmon. Indeed, it's often the highlight of their trip; their whole year in some cases.

Steelheaders, on the other hand, don't care much for salmon, especially Chinooks; they're just too powerful and take too much time to land in fast water. Some guys will fight the fish to the net, but most allow the salmon to break off. Fortunately, the line usually snaps at the hook, so there's little chance of it wrapping around a snag or rock, leaving a trailer that becomes a nuisance to other anglers.

While this might sound cruel and exploitative, it beats risking injury to the fish by fighting it to the net. Oh sure, the salmonid might get a tooth-ache, maybe a sore jaw from the ordeal, but that's a small price to pay for the opportunity to continue heading upriver to fishy paradise.

Steelies don't all look the same. In fact, they can be so colorful, some anglers don't accept they're steelhead, calling them "domestic rainbows" instead. Others are a bit bland, sporting olive green backs spotted in black, silvery sides with a faint, pink stripe running down the side, from the cheek to about the dorsal fin, and white bellies.

Most importantly, a steelies' mouth and gums are white. This is good to know because steelhead are easily confused with coho (black mouth, white gums), and their regulations are different:

- Minimum length for steelhead is 21 inches, and the daily limit is one
- Minimum length for coho is 15 inches and the daily limit is three.

Besides good looks, two other factors endear steelhead to sportsmen: incredible strength and stamina. They owe both to their Western roots. Like Pacific salmon, steelies often climb raging currents and waterfalls to get to the spawning grounds in their home range. Nature ensures they make the trip by endowing them with incredible power, endurance and resolve.

Fallfish

Occupying most of the cold waters in the state, this fish can be found anywhere in the river: holes, rapids, ripples, against the bank, out in the middle, at the heads and tails of pools. While some anglers find them a nuisance—it doesn't take many to ruin a fly—others are grateful they'll hit when the trout won't. Normally smaller than 12 inches in most of their range, the Salmon River regularly coughs up monsters up to 18 inches, and 20-something inchers are rumored to be in the river. The biggest native minnow in the fresh waters of the Northeast, they know their lowly position in aquatic society and become almost as scarce as hen's teeth when the salmon are running.

Catfish

Found in all the lower 48 states, catfish come in all sizes, and rank as one of America's favorite fish. They're often a beginning angler's first catch and an old man's last. Bottom dwellers, they're easy to catch, eagerly hitting anything from nightcrawlers and cut bait to shrimp and commercial stink baits; the more odoriferous, the better.

Two species thrive in the lower river: channel catfish and bullheads. Channel cats hang out between The Sticks at river's end. Typically ranging from three to 10 pounds, a 15-pounder is considered a nice fish, and a 20-something pounder earns bragging rights.

Bullheads typically run one to two pounds; a three-pounder is considered a trophy. Spawning in the Estuary in spring, they're targeted by anglers fishing from the handicap-accessible PAS on the north-western corner of the NY 3 bridge, and on the south bank from Selkirk Shores State Park property on Pine Grove Road.

Fly Fishing

Fly fishing is popular on the lower river. In fact, its devotees (up to 15% of the river's anglers by some estimates) managed to have the state set aside the 0.85 miles of water stretching from the CR 52 bridge in Altmar to the lower reservoir's dam for fly fishing only. And while burly bait and lure anglers often smirk at the thought of whipping a long rod to cast a teeny fly for a spirited stockie, there's nothing wussy about fly fishing on this river.

A wooly bugger in black, chartreuse, or brown is the most popular pattern because it imitates a minnow, leech or nightcrawler, some of a trout's favorite foods. While some anglers fish with dry flies, particularly in summer, they're a specialized, romantic minority. Most come up here for trophy action, and casting tiny flies ain't gonna cut it. You'll get a big one every now and then on a dry, all right, but you'll have to go through countless rough species like fallfish first.

Oh, sure, you'll catch a large salmonid on a dry fly eventually—provided you start at an early age—earning you special bragging rights. But most anglers don't have the time or patience to coax a big fish to rise to drys. Trophies are practical, and a tiny fly doesn't offer enough return for the energy it takes to go for it.

The newest addition to the river's list of productive baits is the yarn fly. Ranging in sophistication from a little strip of brightly colored yarn with a hook on one end, to a multi-colored piece of yarn tied into a marble-sized ball, there's nothing fancy about the things. They can be chuck n' ducked with fly fishing gear or cast with spinning tackle, and bounced on the bottom, worked through pockets and rapids, or suspended below floats in pools.

Float (Bobber) Fishing

One of the most productive ways to catch steelhead is by suspending your bait in the water column with a float. Most every angler on the river uses them some of the time, and some of the most successful guides use them all the time.

The reason float fishing is so productive is because once you figure out what depth the fish are at, and set the float accordingly, you're able to put your offering right in the fish's face with every cast. Steelies are unaccustomed to backing down from things smaller than them, and strike rather than move.

Floats are usually set to keep the bait (egg sacs and three-inch, pink Powerbait Floating Steelhead Worms are popular) anywhere from six inches to a couple of feet off the bottom.

Float Trip (Rowing Down the River)

Without a doubt, the most productive way to fish the lower river is from a drift boat. Also called a McKenzie boat, after the river in Washington where it was developed, its stern is pointed, sides are high, and its bottom arched from bow to stern (the floor is a raised platform). This constant rocker makes the craft maneuverable in rapids.

All the local guides have them. It's the only way they can offer float trips, their bread-and-butter service. In skilled hands, a drift boat can cover all the river's fishy looking spots from Altmar to CR 2A in a day.

Winter drift.

Float trips are more than simply casting baits over the side and going with the flow. You're floating downstream with the rapids all right, but it's a controlled drift. Baits (anything from Kwikfish to Rapalas) running behind the boat, the guide constantly rows against the flow, giving the rapids just enough resistance for them to catch the lures and bring them to life.

All you do is sit there and watch the rods. And if you're not paying attention (the rapids and scenery can be intoxicating) the guide is. Rowing against the current, facing the back of the boat, eyes wide open, he'll bring you back to reality by shouting "fish on" when a rod starts jerking violently, threatening to go over the side.

Another style of float fishing is with bait. The guide drifts the boat into a likely looking spot and anchors. Clients cast into current edges, rapids, flat water, hydraulics, along structure and into pools.

Float trips put you at the mercy of the power company. On typical mornings, summer through winter, the lower river isn't high enough to float a boat until the utility releases water at its hydroelectric plant on the lower reservoir, generally around mid-morning.

Float trips don't normally cover the entire river. Those that launch from Altmar and Pineville generally take out at the Compactor Pool ramp on CR 2A. With good reason: the last three miles of stream get so crowded with anglers, floating through the village of Pulaski amounts to a Kamikaze run.

Indeed, there used to be a ramp off Forest Drive, on Pulaski's west side. "It was closed and gated," claims cousin Staash, "after numerous anglers complained their boats were hit by so many split shots while drifting through town, they thought they were floating through a rifle range."

Drift boat ramps with free launching and parking are available on Bridge Street in Altmar; Centerville Road (off NY 48) in Pineville; CR 2A bridge on the east side of Pulaski and the Selkirk Shores State Park launch on Pine Grove Road, off NY 3.

Taking it to the Bank

Drift boats are expensive and require two to operate (you have to leave cars at put-in and take-out). Most guys don't fish the river enough to justify investing in one and simply buy a good pair of boots instead.

Although the first half-mile or so of stream below the lower dam runs through a gorge and is closed to fishing for safety reasons, and 2.5 miles stretching from Pulaski to the Estuary largely runs through the Douglaston Salmon Run (a pay-to-fish operation owned by former state senator H. Douglas Barkley), the south shore from the Wire Hole about a half-mile upstream of Altmar (angling is prohibited around the hatchery) to a few hundred feet upstream of the US 11 Bridge in Pulaski (roughly 10 miles), and the north bank from the fly-fishing only section in Altmar to roughly a hundred yards below the Black Hole is largely open to free public fishing.

Just about every popular pool has its own parking area or sits within easy walking distance of one. In addition, both sides of the river are lined with beaten paths punctuated with side-trails leading to the water.

Although it's possible to keep dry while fishing from the bank, especially at big pools, landing a salmonid often means getting your feet wet. For one thing, the less line between you and the fish, the easier it is to control the situation. Give the critter too much line and it can thread it between rocks, wrap it around windfalls or even the guy next to you. The line can even bow in the rapids, allowing the whitewater to shake it and work the hook out of the fish's mouth. Even worse is having a trophy break off and tail walk down the rapids while flipping you the fin.

Big fish breaking free are common events on the river. Each escape is unique, etching itself into your imagination for life. After all, the angler who doesn't daydream hasn't been born; and fishing's heartbreaks, like its triumphs, are immortal.

But it's all part of the game. Fortunately, memories of lunkers landed outshine nightmares of trophies lost. Landing one is a major life event. The details splash into your head, emerging later on as daydreams, reminding you how good life is and that there's more to come.

Targeting once in a lifetime trophies is hard work—fish don't get big by being stupid. And while the Salmon River is a great place to cast your fishy dreams, it makes no guarantees. Like a stream flowing through a Hemingway story, it's cold hearted and squeaky clean, as likely to give you cold feet as the trophy of a lifetime, often both at once.

While the fishing can be iffy and the weather cold, a trip to this agitated river is always enlightening. Tumbling through the North-country, digging new channels and filling in the old, it reminds us nothing in nature is permanent. Indeed, if solid rock wears away—even we can't stay.

POPULAR SPOTS

Bottoms Up (Mouth)

In the old days, the 110-foot high Salmon River Falls, roughly 19 miles upstream of the mouth, stopped lake-run fish from going any further. Today, they're blocked about two miles earlier by the dam at Lighthouse Hill Reservoir. That leaves 17-something miles of rapids on the main stream, more than enough to support the river's world-class fishery.

While the whole lower river is trophy water for a variety of fish, species availability depends on where and when you go. During salmon time, the lower in the river you fish the better. The gauntlet of anglers and the rigors of the rapids beat the kings up pretty badly. So the further downstream you fish, the cleaner and healthier the salmon.

Steelhead, on the other hand, are much smaller, find the trip easier, and their numbers grow the further upstream you go.

From its mouth to the last bend, a distance just short of a half-mile, the river runs deep and slow. From ice-out through mid-August, north-erns, smallmouth bass, bullheads and yellow perch thrive throughout the gentle flow. The outlet channel downstream of the lighthouse offers lake-run walleyes in May and June and channel catfish during the salmon run.

Stan Oulette, one of the owners of Deer Creek Motel on NY 3, about three miles north of Port Ontario, fishes between the lighthouse and the last bend in spring and summer, catching enough perch on an average outing (four to six hours) to feed his family of five; and freeze a batch for next time.

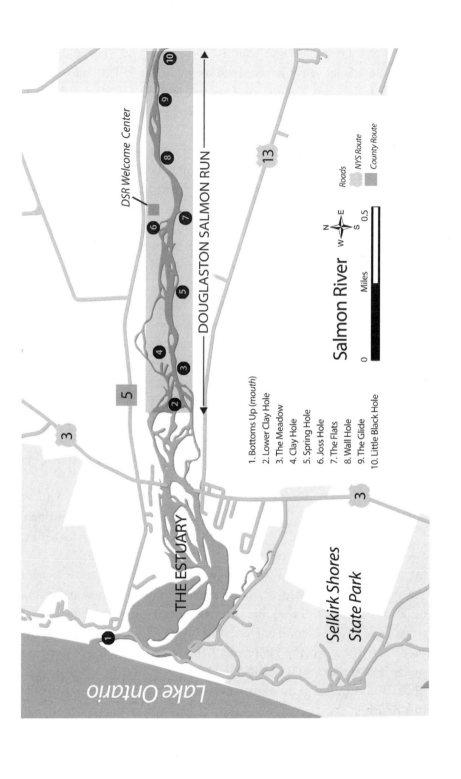

Salmon River

Lake Ontario

THE ESTUARY

Selkirk Shores
State Park

DSR Welcome Center

DOUGLASTON SALMON RUN

1. Bottoms Up (mouth)
2. Lower Clay Hole
3. The Meadow
4. Clay Hole
5. Spring Hole
6. Joss Hole
7. The Flats
8. Wall Hole
9. The Glide
10. Little Black Hole

W ← → E
N
S

Miles
0   0.5

Roads
NYS Route
County Route

"Perch hit minnows best" claims the Vietnam-era Marine. "They'll also take artificial baits like two-inch scented curly-tailed grubs, in-line spinners and spoons. They like worms, too, but you'll have to go through the gobies first," he continues, adding "and they can eat up all your bait. So bring a lot."

Most folks fish with two poles. Three are better, allowing you to cover all the bases: one to fish a minnow on a bobber, another to fish a bait on bottom, and a third to throw a small lure like a two-inch Berkley Power Grub on a jighead.

"Minnows are the charm," argues Oulette. "You just can't go wrong with them. Perch, northerns, black bass, 'rockies,' slab crappies, all the best tasting fish love 'em. I've even caught spring bullheads on buckeyes."

The river below the last bend is also famous for summer bronzebacks. Back in the '60s, when lamprey eels devastated the lake's open water sport fishery, smallies made Selkirk a household word among the state's bass anglers. Unlike the runts commonly caught between the reservoirs and upstream of Redfield, the lower river's bronzebacks typically run from three to four pounds, big enough to write home about.

Smallies rank as the most fisherman-friendly game in the river, just as eager to hit top-water plugs as jigs, minnowbaits as spinnerbaits, streamers as live minnows, crayfish on the rocks, and worms squirming in the mud.

Northern pike rule the stream's bottom end year-round. Named after a deadly, medieval lance, it's one of Europe's most respected fish. It's said that in the Middle Ages, the king would trade a sheep for a pike.

Around here, notherns are the bane of bass anglers because they hit a lot of the same baits. Which would be cool if their teeth weren't sharp enough to cut through monofilament, dacron, fluorocarbon and braided nylon lines like a knife through butter). Big and tough, they're trophies of choice among anglers who like tackling with large, toothy predators. These worthy opponents hangout over weeds, along reeds, under boat docks and windfalls, in the mouths of tributaries, around nooks and crannies in the bank, anywhere there's cover for pike to hide in ambush.

Estuary

Reaching from the last bend in the river at Selkirk upstream to the Douglaston Salmon Run, the Estuary is a large wetland. Much of the south bank borders Selkirk Shores State Park.

Salmon at river's end are generally fresh-run fish, the tastiest in the stream. Although they lose their appetites as soon as they enter the river, they retain their noble cockiness, getting ornerier and ornerier as the river closes in on them, snapping at anything that comes close, including flies.

Bank anglers target them from the south bank off Pine Grove Road, around the state park's boat launch, and from the PAS on the northeastern corner of the NY 3 bridge.

A lot of salmon are caught right from the NY 3 bridges—there are two. It's illegal to fish off them because the highway is so busy, but people try anyway. It's also dangerous because the highway is so heavily traveled, and law enforcement authorities are quick to tell anglers to move. Trails lead down to the river and some folks fish from the bank.

Lodging, boat rentals (motorboats, kayaks and canoes), and slip rentals are available at Salmon River Lighthouse & Marina. Tours of the historic lighthouse, built in 1838, are available on one day's notice.

To get to Pine Grove public boat launch from I-81 exit 36, head west out of Pulaski on NY 13 for four miles, turn south on NY 3, then right about 0.5 mile later onto Pine Grove Road and travel a few hundred yards to the Launch entrance on your right.

Douglaston Salmon Run

Stretching for 2.5 miles through land owned by H. Douglas Barkley, a former NY state senator with 20 years of public service under his belt, the DSR has been a bone of contention from the start. Anglers, particularly professional river guides, were miffed that the senator would charge the public a fee to fish on his property.

The argument made it all the way to the courthouse. Both sides won. The Senator's right to charge the public a fee to walk on his

Paddling the Salmon River at Selkirk.

property—the banks and the river floor—was confirmed. On the other hand, since no one owns the water, it was affirmed anglers have the right to float and fish from a boat or tube, but can't anchor or walk the riverbed on his property without permission.

DSR controls the south bank from a few hundred feet upstream of the Jefferson Street bridge in Pulaski to several hundred feet upstream of the NY 3 bridge in Port Ontario; and the north bank from a little ways below the Black Hole to a few hundred feet above the NY 3 bridge. The south bank in the heart of Pulaski is largely inaccessible because the river skirts a long cliff.

Besides requiring anglers abide by NYS regulations, the DSR has a bunch of its own rules. For instance, the use of more than one hook, or a hook with more than one point, is prohibited and "all trout and Atlantic salmon must be released as quickly as possible . . ." Pacific salmon can be kept in accordance with NYS law.

All the regulations are listed in the free flier "Douglaston Salmon Run Fishing Holes & Trail Map," available at the Welcome Center on Lake Road (CR 5), about a mile west of Pulaski. The brochure contains everything you need to know to fish the DSR ethically and humanely, includes illustrations and detailed descriptions of the salmonids you can expect to catch, and even lists the best months to fish for each species.

Having carved a broad valley through the bottomland, the DSR's stretch of the stream offers a "variety of water types: vast pockets and chutes, deep holes, classic riffles and runs," says manager and river keeper Garrette Brancy.

This is especially important for steelheaders. "Salmon anglers cover one spot and let the salmon come to them," says Brancy. "Steelheaders fish multiple spots."

One of the best things about the DSR is that it educates the fish— it's the relatively gentle first grade in the school of hard knocks they'll face on their way up river. Running wide and relatively shallow for most of its length, it exposes the fish to their initial encounters with the realities of running through a gauntlet of anglers. Entering the downstream end of DSR looking forward, salmonids exit its upper end watching their backs.

Dedicated to providing anglers with a memorable, world class fishing experience, the outfit offers groomed trails to the water, through woods teeming with deer, turkeys and other wildlife; a large heated building to warm up in; a list of professional fishing guides thoroughly familiar with its stretch of river, and the freshest, most attractive and powerful trophies in the drink.

DSR employs river keepers, ensuring angler behavior is the most ethical on the stream.

DSR rates vary throughout the year:

Winter: Dec. 15–March 31
Spring: April 1–May 14
Summer: May 15–Aug. 14
Fall 1: Aug. 15–Sept. 9
Fall 2: Sept. 10–Oct. 31
Fall 3: Nov. 1–Dec. 14

To ensure ". . . every guest has a world class experience," DSR limits the number of anglers on its property to 30 per day from December 15 to March 31 and May 15 to August 14; 250 per day during the peak salmon run, September 10–October 31; and 65 anglers per day the rest of the year.

At press time, a day pass in summer (7 AM to dark) is 75% cheaper than a day pass during the height of the salmon run. Season passes for periods ranging from 3 months to 12 months are available.

Kids under 16 can fish for free when accompanied by a paying adult.

The DSR offers year round lodging, including "two lodges with direct riverside access."

Free walking passes are available at the welcome center for those who want to see the water running through the DSR.

Lower Clay Hole

The lowest hole listed on the Douglaston Salmon Run's publication "Fishing Holes and Trail Map," the Lower Clay is generally recognized as the spot where the river transitions from stream to Estuary. Located

1.3 miles downstream of the Welcome Center, on a well defined trail, it's relatively easy to reach by anglers willing to go the distance; and they're generally few.

The Meadow

Also called the Meadow Run, this area is a favorite of spin fishermen because it's wide open. Salmonids swarm in and mill around trying to figure out how they got themselves into such a tight spot, and what to do next. In the meantime, they react to the irresistible force pulling them forward by hitting just anything careless enough to come within striking distance.

Since they haven't invested too much energy fighting rapids yet, salmonids in the meadow are in top shape. What's more, unlike further upstream, where the fish seek out specific areas to rest and to run, they pretty much run the entire Meadow evenly.

The Meadow is located 1.1 miles downstream of the Welcome Center.

Clay Hole

One of the first spots where fresh-run salmonids need to take a break, this spot holds fish more often than not. Convenient to fish from both banks, it's a favorite angler stop, as well.

This hole is located 0.9 of a mile downstream from the Welcome Center, along a good trail.

Spring Hole

Relatively shallow and wide, this spot averages about three feet deep. Kings are particularly vulnerable because they're easy to spot, if you know what to look for. Their camouflage makes them nearly invisible in rapids. One of the best ways to spot them is to pay attention to small details at the edges of rapids: bubbles that aren't moving, an eye staring at you, even a pale spot in the river.

Joss Hole

Joss Hole, Douglaston Salmon Run.

Squeezed between an island and a cliff on the north bank, the Joss Hole is the only deep spot sandwiched between flat, shallow stretches of river. Fish take a break in its shaded, comforting flow after negotiating the treacherous rapids. The nicest thing about this hole is that it's small, easily covered with fly fishing tackle.

Skirting the north bank a few hundred yards downstream of the welcome center a set of stairs makes getting down to the river easy. The path crosses major deer trails, and sharing the trail with them, even having to stop to let them pass, is one of the DSR's main features.

The Flats

River wide and fairly shallow, the moderate flow of the Flats is ideal holding water for salmonids. The deepest part of the Flats, about four feet, is down the center. The slate and rock floor has an insatiable

The Flats, Douglaston Salmon Run.

appetite for terminal tackle. In-line spinners worked fast enough to run a few inches off bottom will stir all three types of salmon and trophy browns to violence in autumn, and steelhead anytime. Egg sacs are productive fall through spring, and worms have been known to draw chromers and browns in the fall.

The Flats are located just upstream of the lower stairs.

Wall Hole

Located at the bottom of the DSR's eastern stairs, easy access makes this one of the most popular spots on this stretch of the river. Hugging the north bank, averaging about 5.5 feet deep, its floor is carpeted with numerous snags. Fish hold in the edges of the current at the head of the pool. During the run, salmon hold in the edges of the rapids and in the whitewater at the top of the hole.

The Glide

Pouring out of the Little Black Hole, this stretch of rapids is a long way from the road and difficult to get to, so it seldom gets crowded with bank anglers. Drift boats usually drop a line over the side when they float through; sometimes they even go back for a second sweep. While not exactly the hottest steelhead stretch on the river, it's been known to pleasantly surprise anglers who drifted through with a plug over the side.

The Glide marks the spot where both sides of the river slip into the Douglaston Salmon Run.

Little Black Hole

Upstream of the Glide, the river splits in two. Narrow, relatively shallow, the south channel is too dangerous in low water for large fish. The north channel, on the other hand, is much wider and even offers a deep spot: the little Black Hole.

Unfortunately, a steep cliff looms over the north bank, making it impossible to wade from that side. The south shore is fairly level but is part of the DSR and you have to pay the fee.

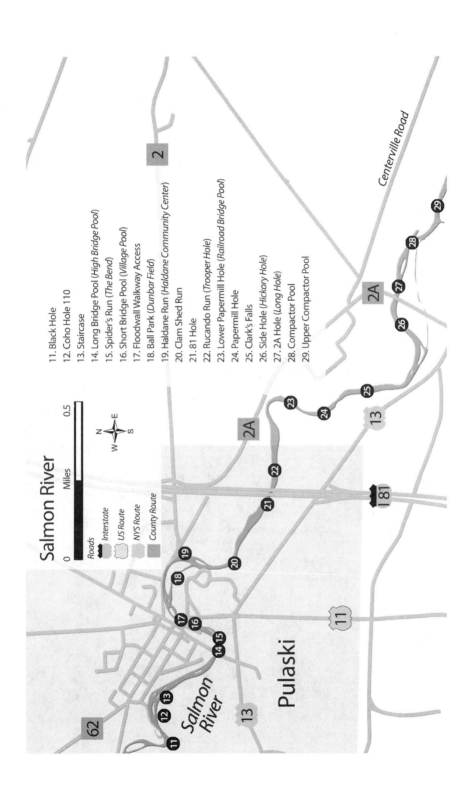

Salmon River

Roads
- ⬛ Interstate
- ⬭ US Route
- ▢ NYS Route
- ▢ County Route

0   Miles   0.5

N W E S

11. Black Hole
12. Coho Hole 110
13. Staircase
14. Long Bridge Pool (*High Bridge Pool*)
15. Spider's Run (*The Bend*)
16. Short Bridge Pool (*Village Pool*)
17. Floodwall Walkway Access
18. Ball Park (*Dunbar Field*)
19. Haldane Run (*Haldane Community Center*)
20. Clam Shed Run
21. 81 Hole
22. Rucando Run (*Trooper Hole*)
23. Lower Papermill Hole (*Railroad Bridge Pool*)
24. Papermill Hole
25. Clark's Falls
26. Side Hole (*Hickory Hole*)
27. 2A Hole (*Long Hole*)
28. Compactor Pool
29. Upper Compactor Pool

Centerville Road

Pulaski

Salmon River

The spot is well worth it, however. Salmon and steelhead move in during the night, making easy pickings for anglers who get there at first light. In addition, fish that break off in the main Black Hole a couple of hundred yards upstream, often beat a hasty retreat down river and end up stopping in the Little Black Hole.

Located about a mile upstream of the DSR Welcome Center, past some good pools and runs, the most exciting way to get to the Little Black Hole is to fish your way up from the DSR. You'll have to cross the river in spots so check to make sure the water's down (315-298-6672). The quickest way there, however, is to wade down from the Black Hole—it's the next pool down.

Black Hole

Like Father like son: River guide Rick Miick, son Brayden, and the boy's first brown trout.

Set into Pulaski's west side, behind (within smelling distance of) the sewage treatment plant on Riverview Drive, this pool is one of the river's biggest and deepest. Its floor drops some 25 feet on the south side (Douglaston Salmon Run property), where a cliff makes bank-fishing and wading impossible in all but its head. However, fishing is easy from the opposite bank. Slowing the river down regardless of water levels, holding fish year-round, easy to get to, boasting a parking lot for over 50 cars, the Black Hole is one of the most popular fishing spots on the stream.

"Pacific salmon make nightly reconnaissance runs upriver in August, getting as far as the Black Hole." claims Rick Miick, one of the stream's most knowledgeable guides. "The majority returns to the lake by morning. But some take a liking to the Black Hole and the rapids below, making this stretch one of your best shots for early season trophies."

"During the run, however" continues Miick, "the 'hole' turns into a three-ring circus: excited salmon rolling on the surface and jumping everywhere; anglers standing in water up to their manhood casting for them; others chasing after them through the rapids, slipping and sliding, even falling in."

As the run progresses, lake-run browns the size of footballs, and steelies twice that big, join the salmon. The browns are there to spawn; the steelies, to feast on fresh caviar.

When November starts knocking leaves off the trees, the salmon run is all but over. A few late bloomers continue entering the stream into November, but their numbers are down drastically and they're pretty beat, scarred with rotting flesh, fins and tails worn down to stubs. Cousin Staash calls them zombies.

Chromers love the hole. They can be caught just about anytime, anywhere, from its head to its tail. Still, there's one hotspot that puts the rest of the pool to shame. Located on the south side, 20 to 40 feet above pool's end, it always holds fish; the biggest in the hole, for that matter. They find it particularly attractive in winter.

Steelhead occupy the hole year-round, but are most plentiful autumn through spring. Atlantics come through in summer, Pacific salmon and browns come through in autumn. Smallmouth bass up to four pounds are plentiful in summer.

Just about any small, white, in-line spinner will catch steelhead, but they're particularly prejudiced against the old Luhr-Jensen Fire Plug. Unfortunately, the lure isn't made anymore and it's getting hard to find. A small Flatfish in silver, fluorescent/red or fluorescent /orange is a good substitute.

To get to the Black Hole from US 11 north in downtown Pulaski, take a left at the light just past the movie theater onto Lake Street (CR 5), another left on Bridge Street four blocks later, then right almost imme-diately onto Riverview Drive. The parking lot is on the right.

Coho Hole

The next hole up, the Coho Hole, is a little controversial: some say it's the hole skirting the cliff on the north bank, others say it's the biggest pocket in the rapids running along the south side of the island. One thing's for sure, the only way you can fish it on foot is from the DSR (ask for directions and where to cross at the welcome center). You can get to it by crossing the river at the Staircase but make sure you have a DSR pass, or face being asked to leave by the outfit's river keepers.

Difficult to reach, this hole doesn't get too much angling pres-sure. But it's always worth a try because its relatively gentle flow invites salmonids to take a short break after climbing up from the Black Hole.

Swinging a streamer through the current is usually productive.

Staircase

From the Long Bridge Pool to the Black Hole, the river drops gently into pools and pockets called the Staircase. Its location between two of the stream's largest pools keeps the Staircase well stocked with fish. The south shore, DSR property, is inaccessible to bank anglers because of a steep cliff. The north side is wader-friendly.

During high water, the Staircase is a long, wide rapid, impossible to wade to get to the river's deep edges along the cliff on the south shore.

On the other hand, when the water's low, the Staircase's clarity, pockets, rapids and wide open spaces make it a wading angler's fantasy.

Winter transforms the Staircase into a visual feast. Ice formations cling to the cliff like chandeliers; shelves of ice reach out into the pools; ice skirts the waterline along rapids like fine lace; and icicles hang from root balls and fallen timber on the bank.

The best fishing is during first light because the area loads up with anglers around dawn and they pretty much fish the place out by 9 AM. Still, fresh-run fish, drop-backs and refugees fleeing the frenzy upstream keep the Staircase well stocked all day long.

Getting here is easy for the able-bodied. A handicapped parking spot big enough for two cars is on Forest Drive. A primitive trail several hundred feet long leads from the parking area to the water's edge (how anglers without the use of legs or arms are expected to get to the river over the rough terrain is beyond this author) .

Long Bridge Pool (High Bridge Pool)

Named after the long, tall bridge on the west side of Pulaski, this hole is about 20 feet deep and a couple of hundred yards long. A cliff skirts its south shore (largely DSR property) and there's no bank access to the water on that side.

But that's all right because the north shore is open to everyone without discrimination. Big enough to offer salmonids a sense of security after struggling up the Staircase, even when anglers ring its banks, this pool always has fish, including lunker smallies in summer. It gets crowded at times but there's usually enough room to go around. Still, if you want to fish with fly-fishing gear (a lot of guys do, even with bait), hone your rollcasting skills.

Located below the South Jefferson Street bridge on the village's west side, this hole is separated from the mainland by a channel that's about 20 feet wide and barely deep enough in spots to wet your feet during low water, three-something feet deep during water releases, around 11 AM on weekdays. Salmonids have been observed in this channel, but only rarely.

Street parking is available on South Jefferson and James Streets.

Remains of an Old mill at the Long Bridge Pool, Pulaski.

Spider's Run (The Bend)

Path along Spider's Run, between the bridges, Pulaski.

This is my favorite spot. Old timers call it the Bend, but you seldom hear it called that anymore . . . so I'd like to rename it Spider's Run.

Beginning at the foot of the Short Bridge Pool, this set of rapids takes a break in a shallow pool about 50 yards downstream, revs up into impressive whitewater at the tail-out, and careens down a gentle slope along a steep cliff for a couple of hundred yards, coming to rest in the Long Bridge Pool.

Visible from the US 11 and the South Jefferson Street bridges, Spider's Run is ignored by average anglers because it's largely rapids, and in the heart of the village to boot. They can't imagine fish could find comfort there.

Big mistake! Salmonids are made for rapids—they're born and die there. Bubbles, broken surfaces and back currents in the hydraulics behind the boulders are rich in oxygen, provide good cover, and make swimming in place easy for fish when they need to rest.

Averaging about 20 feet wide and four feet deep during low water, Spider's Run adds about 10 feet to its width and a couple of feet to its depth during high water events.

The lower half is the most productive stretch. Coming out of the High Bridge Pool, salmonids entering Spider's Run are immediately met by its highly oxygenated water. Giddy, they barrel carelessly forward. That's all right under cover of night when fishing is prohibited. When it's permitted a half-hour before dawn, however, the unsuspecting salmonids run into swarms of hooks.

Still, they gotta get upstream, making this spot highly productive even between noon and dusk. By that time, most of the experienced guys have limited-out and left. However, fish escaping anglers ringing the popular pools above and below Spider's Run send a steady stream of fish into its rapids throughout the day.

Short Bridge Pool (Village Pool)

One of the river's most popular spots because of its high visibility (the U.S.11 bridge crosses over it) and easy access, this pool is in the heart of the village of Pulaski. Most weekends during the run, the bridge holds what cousin Staash calls "the cheering section"—pedestrians, up to three thick in spots, leaning against the railings, egging on, sometimes jeering at, the anglers below.

Stretching over 100 yards, directed by a concrete wall on the north bank, carpeted in cobblestones on the other side, the north shore is open to public fishing without discrimination. The south bank runs behind businesses; it's a good idea to get permission to fish there.

Deep enough to tame the river's rapids momentarily, wide enough to boast fish-holding edges on both sides of the current, relatively safe to fish, this hole is always graced with anglers. It's the ideal place for guys who like to fish in convenient locations and in the company of others.

(While company isn't exactly what most anglers look for, it's a good thing for rookies on this river. After all, the best way to pick up fishing tips [each stream is different] and safety advice is by watching and talking to regulars.)

Located in the heart of town, the Pulaski Fishing Parking Lot on Maple Avenue (the first right after the movie theater on US 11 North) grants easy access to the head of the Short Bridge Pool via the floodwall (see below). A smaller lot is located at the end of the pool, on the other side of the river, between retail establishments on Salina Street (US 11).

Floodwall Walkway Access

Constructed in the heart of Pulaski in 2013, along Eye of the Needle, the river's tallest rapids, the walkway opens a tempting spot formerly blocked to foot anglers by a cliff.

Located at the head of the Town Pool, the walkway hugs the rapids at the northeastern corner of the US 11 Bridge. Before the walkway's construction, bank anglers fishing just upstream of the bridge invariably lost their fish when trophies charged under the structure, where anglers couldn't follow.

"By providing access to the base of the class III rapids feeding the Town Pool, the walkway provides a remedy for the frustration anglers used to suffer while fishing this village hot spot," claims Miick.

To get there, follow the directions to the Short Bridge Pool above.

Ball Park (Dunbar Field)

Skirting the south bank within earshot of downtown Pulaski, this site offers easy access to the productive pocket water in the southern channel between the mainland and Pulaski's largest island.

This is an ideal spot for early risers because the crack of dawn usually sees the water down and fish scattered all over the rapids. The majority gets caught out within a couple of hours. Still, when the salmon are running, they move through pretty steady all day long in both directions—regardless of water levels; sometimes on their own, sometimes with anglers hot on their tails.

At the Ball Park, Pulaski.

Located on Lewis Street (turn north after crossing the railroad tracks on NY 13), a few hundred feet upstream of the Short Bridge Pool, the park offers a drift boat launch and parking for dozens of cars.

Haldane Run (Haldane Community Center)

Across the river, and a little upstream of the above site, this stretch of pockets runs from the head of Dunbar Field to the bottom of the 81 hole. Night-running fish pack into the area but its rapids and pockets get picked quickly by early-morning anglers. Still, steady streams of salmon, sprinkled with chromers and browns, run when the water is up.

This is a great spot for casting lures and streamers.

Located off Maple Avenue Extension, on the east side of Pulaski, the center offers easy access to the north bank and lots of parking.

Clam Shed Run

To the untrained eye, the rapids between I-81 and the top of the Ball Park seem barren, a waste of good water. It only stands to reason that if you cast to a spot and the current carries your bait away before it can hit bottom, the water's too fast. After all, fish can't live in places where they spend every moment fighting current, right?

Wrong.

Rapids are a little more complicated than that. While they may spit and foam in a bubbling rage on the surface, down below they're moving slow. Everything from boulders and fallen timber to holes, drop-offs, twisting channels, river bends, and a host of other factors slow the flow on the bottom. Add a salmonids' streamlined shape and camouflaging spots (which look like bubbles) to the equation, and you come up with a critter and habitat that are made for each other.

81 Hole

The I-81 Hole starts directly below the eastern edge of the interstate's southbound lane and stretches for several hundred feet downstream. First light catches salmon climbing Haldane Run, forcing them

Guide John Kopy holds a steelie caught at the 81 Hole.

through a gauntlet of early-morning anglers. Those that make it to the hole find its deceiving depths reassuring for a moment or two. That's all it takes for the rain of hooks to prick their bubbles. Still, salmonids often occupy the pool at dawn. During high water, fish hang out in the backwashes of the abutments.

The south side of the hole is easy to access by hiking a few hundred yards upstream from Dunbar Field (see above). Start at the tailout and work your way up to the pool below the expressway's southbound lane.

The North side is accessible by hiking upstream from the Haldane Community Center (see above) or downstream from the Trooper Hole (see below).

Rucando Run (Trooper Hole)

Stretching from the Lower Paper Hole downstream to I-81, Rucando Run is a long set of rapids punctuated by a series of pockets along the north shore. It's so shallow and featureless that few anglers give it a moment's thought.

And that's the beauty of the place. Generally devoid of packs of attacking anglers, salmonids don't see Rucando Run as particularly dangerous, push through its rapids and rest in its pockets fearlessly, even in broad daylight. From a fish's point of view, its channels, hydraulics and backwashes offer heavenly respites from the challenges they overcame in the angler-lined rapids downstream.

Indeed, in low water, it's the safest passage in this section of the stream. When the water's up, however, the run becomes part of a river-wide rapid.

Named after John Rucando, a retired, local guide originally hailing from New Jersey, the stretch deserves its name. His knowledge of the river and knack for taking fish in unlikely spots made him one of the stream's most popular guides in his time.

Most of the river runs along the north shore. During low water, there's a small hole that clings to the north bank about mid-way between the Lower Paper Hole and the interstate. Some call it the Trooper Hole after the barracks that used to be on CR 2A. Most don't call it anything at all. Small enough for an untrained eye to miss, it's the quietest spot on the run, a welcome respite for fish climbing the rapids.

Rucando Run takes some effort to get to on foot because of its distance from the road, but its generosity during salmon season makes the hike worthwhile. It doesn't take long to put a salmon on the stringer, nor for the place to pour into your imagination, right into your list of favorites.

From I-81 north exit 36, head south (right) on NY 13 for a mile, turn left on CR 2A, cross the river, travel about 0.5 a mile, cross the railroad tracks and park in the gravel lot on the other side of the road. Walk the tracks to the far side of the railroad trestle (about 400 paces), take the path down to the water and walk downstream to the rapids at the end of the Lower Papermill Hole.

Lower Papermill Hole (Railroad Bridge Pool)

A stone's throw downstream of the railroad trestle on Pulaski's east end (off CR 2A), this hole's deep, north side is inaccessible from the bank because of a cliff. The south shore, on the other hand, has a trail going down to the river from the corner of the bridge. Sparsely planted with brush and wildflowers, it's open enough for easy back-casting. Physically exerting to access because of its distance from the road and the steep bank down to the water, this deep, slow moving hole offers elbow room during the week, and on weekend afternoons.

To get there, follow the directions to the above site. It's the big hole a few hundred feet downstream of the railroad bridge.

Papermill Hole

Located behind the Felix Schoeller North America, Inc. plant on CR 2A, upstream of the railroad trestle, this is another one of the river's deepest, largest pools. During the run, salmon find some relief from the rain of hooks, as well as resting spots in the eddies below the cliffs on the south bank. Egg sacs fished slow and deep at the head catch steelies and an occasional brown from October through April. Skamania respond with extreme prejudice to in-line spinners cast upstream and retrieved rapidly in summer, and at a moderate clip October through April. Streamers swung through the current drive steelies to violence year-round. This hole's quiet water is a great place to cast dry flies like caddis and mayflies on quiet summer evenings.

Follow the directions to Rucando's Run above, but instead of crossing the trestle, head down the steep trail on the left just before the bridge. You'll be at the Papermill Hole when you get to bottom.

Clark's Falls

A few hundred feet upstream of the Papermill Pool, Clark's Falls punctuates the river like a two-foot high step in the rapids. Nothing serious for salmonids. In fact, most swim right through the chute in the center without ever being seen by the outside world. Some always take the hard way and jump it, however. The highly oxygenated pockets below the falls, and behind boulders in nearby rapids often hold salmon at first light.

Clarks Falls shows up on satellite images.

Side Hole (Hickory Hole)

Located at the bend downstream of the CR2A bridge, this hole is shallow at the head, growing deeper and wider as it rounds the bend. Usually pretty quiet during the day, sundown pulls the trigger, sending a steady stream of fish shooting through the rapids on both ends of the hole straight through to first light.

This spot is easiest to fish from the south bank, during low water.

2A Hole (Long Hole)

Moving out of the Hickory Hole, salmon encounter shallow rapids again. The next break they get from heavy current is the CR 2A Hole, a few hundred yards upstream.

Called the Long Hole by old timers, it starts at the downstream side of its namesake bridge. The upper half of the 2A Hole is best fished from the north bank, the closer to the bridge the better. Fish rest under

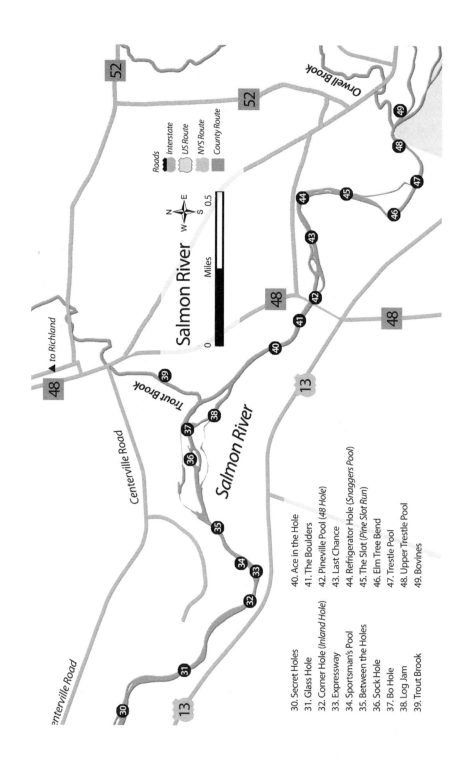

Salmon River

Roads
Interstate
US Route
NYS Route
County Route

N W E S

Miles
0   0.5

Orwell Brook

Trout Brook

Salmon River

Centerville Road

Centerville Road

to Richland

30. Secret Holes
31. Glass Hole
32. Corner Hole (Inland Hole)
33. Expressway
34. Sportsman's Pool
35. Between the Holes
36. Sock Hole
37. Bo Hole
38. Log Jam
39. Trout Brook

40. Ace in the Hole
41. The Boulders
42. Pineville Pool (48 Hole)
43. Last Chance
44. Refrigerator Hole (Snaggers Pool)
45. The Slot (Pine Slot Run)
46. Elm Tree Bend
47. Trestle Pool
48. Upper Trestle Pool
49. Bovines

the road and in its shadow, swimming up and down the pool. Since it's difficult to impossible for bank anglers to harass them under the structure, the fish come out of its shadow refreshed and emboldened. This hole is best fished from the north shore because that's where the water's deepest.

Compactor Pool

This pool throws folks because it moves so much.

Stretching from the CR 2A bridge to a little ways above the old railroad trestle (one of its old cut-limestone piers still stands in the river like a confused sentinel from the past), this pool used to have a lot of fishable water. Not anymore, possibly because the village put in a transfer station on the north bank that may have changed the flow. Nowadays it's a shallow, stream-wide ripple in low water, rapids when the river's high. About the only spot worth casting to is the ephemeral hole at the base of the aging trestle support. Snowmelt and heavy rains tend to dig it out momentarily, but the river always fills it in again.

This spot has two ramps on the same side of the river: a paved one at the northeastern corner of the CR 2A bridge, and a hard surface launch about 50 yards further upstream. There's parking for about 25 rigs.

Upper Compactor Pool

This pool is right where it says it is: upstream of the Compactor Pool. Roughly 600 feet long, averaging about five feet deep, it owes its popularity to its distance from CR 2A; far enough in the woods so you can't see or hear the highway. Indeed, the hike discourages most anglers. Those who decide to make the trek during the run are encouraged— and guided—about half-way there by the whooping and hollering they hear coming from upstream. In winter, the deep silence of the place is punctuated by the splashes of steelhead fighting to get off the hook.

It's best to fish this spot from the south bank. You can fish from the north bank, but it's high, the fish normally hide there, and you risk spooking them, resulting in the anglers on the other side giving you the evil eye and the finger.

Compactor Pool.

The easiest way to get there is to park at the shoulder on the south side of the CR 2A bridge and walk upstream. If you prefer the safety of a parking lot, use the Compactor Pool's fishing access site on the other side of the river.

Secret Holes

Among the river's smaller pools, these spots will only fit about a half-dozen anglers each, eight in a pinch. Skamania chase streamers through the rapids at its head and tail, and enthusiastically slurp dries in its quiet middle. Autumn sees salmon rolling on the surface, striking any streamer that's arrogant enough to think it has a right to be there.

These are great spots to cast streamers and minnowbaits.

Get there by parking at the old silo on NY 13 (0.8 miles east of CR 2A) and follow the trail (there are several at the road that lead to a major one). The holes are downstream.

A word of warning: the gravel along the edges has a tendency to give if you get too close.

Glass Hole

This hole averages about five feet deep during low water. Its deepest area is a slot running down its length, along the south shore. Fishable from both banks, the south shore is most popular because it's closest to the slot—and you don't have to worry about being stuck on the wrong side of the river if the water comes up.

Located about a half-mile downstream of the Sportsman's Pool (see below).

Corner Hole (Inland Hole)

Located at the bend just downstream of the Sportsman's Pool, this hole is about seven feet deep under low water levels. Its carpet of sharp-edged shale has an insatiable appetite for split shot. Rigs weighed down with pencil lead or Slinkies survive more casts.

Besides waking up in the morning to its own fresh run of fish, the Corner Hole's stock is replenished all day long by fish running upriver from the Secret Hole or breaking out of the Sportsman's Hole just upstream.

Expressway

This set of rapids runs between the Corner Hole and Sportsman's Pool, two of the river's most popular fishing spots. During the run, cocky, fresh-run Pacific salmon charge this stretch of whitewater all day long.

Early morning sees the greatest number of clean fish. Having spent a relatively hassle-free night in the river, salmonids run the Expressway confidently. Anglers who arrive around dawn often have their limits by 8 AM.

"You'd get your limit a lot sooner if the salmon and trout didn't take so long to come in," explains cousin Staash.

Sportsman's Pool

This is another one of the river's most popular holes. It would be *numero uno* if it wasn't so far from the road (you have to walk about 400 paces to get to the water). Although not quite as deep as the Black Hole, it's much longer, and offers parking and access on both sides of the river. Weekends during the run normally see its banks crowded but the hole is big enough to hold a lot of fish and anglers, and everyone generally gets along. Most guys fish this spot by chuck-n-duckin' egg sacs and single artificial eggs.

After the run, the hole still gets a lot of pressure but there's usually enough room for anglers to swing streamers through the current in the upper part; cast and retrieve them slowly in the quieter water. Three-inch pink worms or egg sacs fished below floats, and minnowbaits and in-line spinners also catch a lot of chromers from November through March.

Public access to the hole's south bank, complete with parking for about 50 cars, is on NY 13, 2.9 miles south of I-81 exit 36.

Public access with parking for the north bank is on Centerville Road, about 2.5 miles east of its intersection with CR2A.

Between the Holes

The stretch of pocket water between the Sportsman's Pool and the Sock Hole can be surprisingly productive during the run. Cast egg sacs or egg patterns on your way upstream, and swing streamers on your way down. Cousin Staash claims there have been times when he didn't make it to the Sock Hole because so many fish were in the rapids on the way up.

Sock Hole

The next hole up from the Sportsman's Pool, this spot is full of surprises. Kind of small, its size fools a lot of guys, discouraging them from even trying. Averaging a little over five feet deep during low water, it's one of those pools that never seems to run out of fish. During the run, most of the salmonids that move in during the night are usually caught out by coffee time the next morning. But they're replaced throughout the day by fresh-run fish and drop-backs.

Get there from the Sportsman's Pool by walking upstream about three quarters of a mile.

Bo Hole

Set at the foot of an island, this hole gives fish a much needed breather after they run a quarter-mile or so of rapids getting here from the Sock Hole. Facing two channels, they mill around in the "Bo" for a spell trying to decide which route to take upstream.

Running along the north side of the island, the main channel's high volume of water and, more importantly, the scent of Trout Brook, are hard to resist. Feeding the river a few hundred feet above the "Bo," Trout Brook is an important salmonid spawning ground, drawing fish into the upper channel year-round.

Log Jam

Located in the southern channel going around the island upstream of the Bo Hole, the Log Jam's collection of holes, pockets, bends, undercut banks, and windfalls offers salmonids a variety of options for every contingency. If the fish get spooked out of the rapids, they can hold tight to the bank or even under it. If the Bo Hole's open water leaves them feeling exposed and vulnerable, they can hide under its windfalls, ripples and deep current. And if the fish are hungry, all they have to do is hold in the edges of the current, open their mouths and the current will just about hand-feed them a cornucopia ranging from salmon and trout eggs to insects and nightcrawlers.

Relatively difficult to get to, the Log Jam Hole is a peaceful place. Steeped in silence, normally free of careless men whipping long rods, it must be approached cautiously, without any surprises. Sudden movements, unnatural vibrations and careless splashing will give the fish lockjaw for the better part of an hour, if not the rest of the day.

Trout Brook

Gurgling out of the foothills of the Tug Hill Plateau, one of the state's most remote regions, this skinny creek stays cool by snaking under a canopy of forest and brush for its 10-mile existence, feeding the Salmon River downstream of Pineville. While some of its salmonids trace their roots to the Salmon River hatchery, most of its fish are wild. Boasting all the popular species, the DEC considers it the most productive steelhead spawning site in the Salmon River drainage.

The state offers 5.3 miles of public fishing rights on the stream. Its last half-mile is most popular, going from a fast moving, blue-ribbon trout stream at the CR 48 bridge about a mile north of Pineville, to a relatively deep, slowly meandering stream at its mouth.

Only averaging about 15 feet wide, it's easiest to fish with fly-fishing gear.

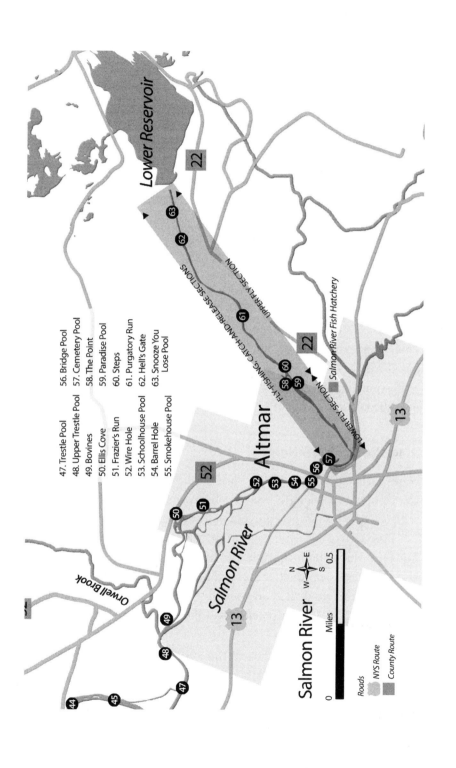

47. Trestle Pool
48. Upper Trestle Pool
49. Bovines
50. Ellis Cove
51. Frazier's Run
52. Wire Hole
53. Schoolhouse Pool
54. Barrel Hole
55. Smokehouse Pool
56. Bridge Pool
57. Cemetery Pool
58. The Point
59. Paradise Pool
60. Steps
61. Purgatory Run
62. Hell's Gate
63. Snooze You Lose Pool

Lower Reservoir

Orwell Brook

Altmar

Salmon River

Salmon River Fish Hatchery

FLY-FISHING, CATCH-AND-RELEASE SECTIONS

UPPER FLY SECTION

LOWER FLY SECTION

Salmon River

Roads

NYS Route

County Route

Miles
0   0.5

Ace in the Hole

Often called Ace Hole by anglers with a sense of humor, this spot is located at the bend downstream of the 48 Hole. Close enough to the road for reasonably fit anglers to reach without breathing hard, it can get crowded but doesn't generally see the numbers that holes closer to the highway do.

A fairly long pool, finding a spot to fish on the Ace Hole isn't usually a problem. You might have to settle for a position you feel is less than ideal, but a short wait usually frees-up the place you want to be.

This hole always holds fish and is a good spot to cast crankbaits and spinners, and fly-fish with streamers.

The Boulders

This boney stretch of water is located at the bend below the Pineville Pool. Its pockets hold salmon and browns in early autumn, and steelies fall through spring. Walt Geryk, one of the stream's most popular professional guides, says: "When the river's down, there's a lot of cover in the Boulders section."

Pineville Pool (48 Hole)

Named after the highway that crosses it, this hole is one of the river's most popular. Its length and width draw salmonids; and they, along with the easy access, lure anglers.

Productive year-round, its hot spots move with the seasons. Summer finds fish throughout the hole and fly-fishing with dry flies like caddis and mayflies is productive for Skamania and river browns. Nymphs cast upstream and drifted down with the current, and streamers swung through the pool are also effective. Finally, small silver spoons and spinners are deadly.

During the run, one part of the pool is just about as good as any other, especially on weekends. Just about any spot will do. Since most anglers wouldn't dream of drifting through the heavy crowds, guys in tall boots usually have the place pretty much to themselves. Just wiggle in anywhere you can. You'll score eventually.

The water downstream of the bridge is the spot to fish during winter. The side doesn't matter. Indeed, during periods of extremely harsh weather with heavy snowfall, the section of CR 48 that crosses the river, from NY 13 to Sheepskin Road, might not even get plowed. When that happens, you'll have to park on NY 13 or Sheepskin Road and hike in. Anglers familiar with the Northcountry winters, especially those who want to get a jump on things immediately after a heavy snowfall, keep snowshoes in their vehicles.

The nicest thing about winter fishing in the hole is it's relatively easy. Just cast into the current and let it carry the offering downstream. When it reaches the end of the line, whip the rod back, sending the fly upstream, then whip the rod forward, casting the line across the current and let the bait swing down. The fish almost invariably hit when the fly swings to the edge of the current below you and turns to face upstream.

If nothing strikes, just whip the rod back forcefully upriver (the streamer will lift out of the water and fly behind you), then flick your wrist so the rod faces the other side of the river and whip the fly out. With a little practice, you'll be swinging streamers through the current almost effortlessly, without false casts, just a couple of smooth movements of the rod.

Just about any brown, chartreuse or black streamer swung through the current will result in a vicious attack by a steelie, giving you a clear understanding of the river's most popular phrase: "The drug is in the tug."

Last Chance

The channels running around the island just upstream of the Pineville Bridge are called the Last Chance. No one knows—or admits knowing— where the name came from. Rumor has it the name goes back to early days of the snagging era, when the CR 48 bridge was the line dividing the snagging section from the single-hook stretch.

The north channel is generally the most productive. But you have to get there early, before the anglers who launched in Altmar earlier in the morning start banging the river floor with their oars and the bottoms of their boats.

Refrigerator Hole (Snaggers Pool)

Located at the bend where the river first meets Sheepskin Road (below the entrance to the Trestle Pool North access road), this hole is named after a discarded refrigerator that used to be on the bank. An organized clean-up of the area hauled it away—but the name stayed.

Averaging about five feet deep, salmon load up in the hole early in the morning, especially in the small pocket at the tail . . . and so do anglers. Chromers, and an occasional brown hold along the north bank during high water.

This hole is difficult to reach on foot because its south bank is about 0.5 mile upstream from CR 48; while the north bank is steep, and springs make it soggy and slippery

The Slot (Pine Slot Run)

Set midway in the rapids running between the Refrigerator Hole and Elm Tree Hole, this long cut in the stream's floor is the only distinct feature for a quarter mile in both directions. Nothing extraordinary, it nonetheless draws fish because it's the deepest spot around.

Park on the shoulder of Centerville Road at the entrance to the Trestle Pool North access, climb down the hill and walk upstream for about 0.25 miles.

Elm Tree Bend

Rounding the second bend 0.5 miles downstream of the Trestle Pool, the river pours into some deep pockets. Salmon and steelhead hold in the hydraulics (where the river flows back on itself) and move in the edges of the current.

Trestle Pool

Dug by rapids squeezing between the abutments of an old railroad trestle, and wrapping around the pier in the middle of the river, this pool averages about eight feet deep and is well over 100 yards long. It's so popular, the authorities built PAS with parking lots on both sides.

Trestle Pool.

All the popular techniques work here. It gets crowded during the run so you'll only be able to cast out directly in front of you. The best equipment to use in the lower two-thirds of the hole is spinning tackle. Fly-fishing with streamers is generally productive at the head, spring through autumn.

The north PAS is easiest to reach. Get there from Pineville by heading north on CR 48. Cross the bridge, turn right on Sheepskin Road, then right again, about 0.5 mile later onto the hard surface road (old railroad grade) and travel to the end, about 0.5 mile.

The south PAS is on NY 13, about a mile east of Pineville. There's parking for about 10 cars. You'll have to walk about a third of a mile to get to the water.

Upper Trestle Pool

Located at the bend a few hundred feet upstream of the Trestle Pool, this hole was dug by rapids rounding a bend. Orwell Brook feeds the river at the head of the pool. By the time the water reaches the bend, the brook's scent, dispersed throughout the pool, is strong enough to hook the fish's curiosity, momentarily distracting them from their determination to get upstream. They mill around for a short time in the pool trying to figure out what smells so good.

On the other hand, the hole is the first big water that fish that have spawned in Orwell Brook encounter on their return trip downstream, and many feel safe enough to take a break.

And while the spent Pacific salmon milling around waiting to die are usually so beat-up they look like zombies, they still have a lot of power—and a cocky attitude.

The nicest thing about this spot, however, is its proximity to the lower Trestle Pool. Far enough away to look tiny through the trees, most anglers opt to wiggle their way into the excited mob of anglers circling the lower pool than take a chance on quieter, less popular Upper Trestle Pool.

Bovines

Starting around the bend below Ellis Cove, this short stretch of the river is named for its slow, channel-like pace during low water. The skinniest section of the lower river, the hole is deepest along the southern edge where it runs under the bank.

Salmon generally zip right through, but injured and exhausted fish will rest and take cover under the bank. Steelhead hold in the head and tail in autumn, hug the south bank in winter, hang out on bottom along the current's edges in spring, and take cover from the summer's sunlight in the deep middle.

A trail leads down to the hole from the upstream end of the Ellis Cove parking area on CR 52.

Ellis Cove

Ellis Cove, County Route 52.

Hugging the side of the road, Ellis Cove is the widest, deepest arm of the river after it breaks up into three channels a little less than a mile downstream of Altmar. Several holes punctuate its floor. Be prepared to add and remove splitshot as you work your way through it.

Its proximity to the road draws a lot of attention and it gets pretty crowded during the run; and hosts an angler or two most of the rest of the time. Still, it offers a lot of choice water, offering a lot of room to go around.

Frazier's Run

This relatively narrow set of rapids feeds Ellis Cove. It doesn't look like much to the human eye, and it really isn't most of the time. During the run, however, slick salmon will hold in the rapids and pockets playing hide-and-go-seek. It's always worth walking stealthily upstream a little ways after fishing Ellis Cove, and swinging a streamer on your way down. During the run, cast to anything long and dark that looks out of the ordinary.

Wire Hole

Heading to or from Altmar the back way, along Bridge Street (CR 52), the transition at Tar Hill Road always seems to have cars parked on the shoulder. That's because the best way to get to the north bank of the lower Wire Hole is to follow the power lines to the water.

This long, wide hole averages about five feet deep. And while its water is constantly moving, it's deep and slow enough to hold fish without too much effort on their part.

Get there from Altmar by heading north on Bridge Street (CR 52) for a couple of hundred yards or so to its intersection with Tar Hill Road, park on the shoulder at the fork in the road, and follow the overhead wires to the river.

Schoolhouse Pool

Located behind the old schoolhouse in Altmar, now the Tailwater Lodge, this hole is another one that never seems to run out of fish.

While its south bank is controlled by the lodge, and anglers are at the mercy of the innkeeper, it's a large pool and its north bank is open to free public fishing without any strings attached. Its size makes it a good spot to cast spinners and plugs.

Get there by parking in one of the lots at the CR 52 bridge and walking the path downstream along the north side of the river. Or follow the power line mentioned above and head upstream.

Barrel Hole

Words and phrases often mean different things to different folks. This hole is a perfect example. Depending on who you talk to, the Barrel Hole is either the set of rapids stretching from the CR 52 Bridge to the Schoolhouse Pool, or simply the river-wide pocket in the rapids about hundred feet below the bridge. (This author prefers the second choice.)

Large and deep enough to offer salmonids a tiny degree of security after running the relatively shallow, cover-free rapids upstream of the Schoolhouse Pool, this slick spot in the river is always lined with anglers. The hole's center is the deepest part and usually has the most fish—and anglers.

However, the "Barrel's" head and tail are also productive, particularly just before dark and at first light. By this point in the run, salmonids are so close to Beaverdam Brook, it's intoxicating. Determined to get there come man or low water, they charge forward. Feeling their oats, unwilling to appear weak to potential mates that may be watching, they strike anything bite-sized that gets in their way.

Smokehouse Pool

Directly below the downstream side of the bridge in Altmar, this pool is actually the tail end of the Bridge Pool (see below). Named after a smokehouse that used to stand on the bank nearby, it's the furthest point upstream on the lower river where regular fishing, and keeping your catch, are allowed.

"The average man on the stream wants to take home a fish," claims cousin Staash. "And the later in the season, the more salmon there are upstream. So the closer to the hatchery you fish from mid-September through mid-October, the better your chances of scoring. Since the Smokehouse Pool is as far upriver as you can fish with regular tackle, and keep your catch, it's always a good bet during the run."

"Be prepared for combat fishing," advises cousin Staash.

FLY-FISHING, CATCH-AND-RELEASE SECTIONS

From the bridge in Altmar upstream to the No-Fishing sign dangling from a wire in the gorge, a little ways below the Lighthouse Hill Reservoir dam, angling is restricted to certain dates and catch and release fly-fishing only on the two short sections of river mentioned below:

LOWER FLY SECTION: Running from the CR 52 bridge in Altmar upstream 0.25 mile to the marked boundary at Beaverdam Brook (it drains the Salmon River Hatchery), this stretch is open to fishing from September 15 through May 15.

UPPER FLY SECTION: Stretching from a marked boundary upstream of the New York State Fish Hatchery property to the marked boundary 0.6 miles upstream at the Lighthouse Hill Reservoir tailrace, this section is open to fishing from April 1 to November 30.

Fishing is restricted to conventional fly fishing tackle: fly rod, fly reel and fly line.

Only artificial flies can be used for bait.

Fishing is prohibited outside of the open season, although fishing is allowed, as noted above, in either the Lower or Upper section year-round.

All fish must be released immediately without unnecessary injury.

Only floating fly lines are permitted from May 1 through August 31.

In addition, there are restrictions on leaders, number of hooks, attractors, amount and placement of weight. For instance, "From May 1 through August 31: the use of supplemental weight such as split shot, sinkers, metal leaders, twist-ons, or swivels attached to the leader, tippet, fly line or fly is prohibited."

And there's more. Check the "Special Regulations by Section for the Salmon River and Tributaries (Oswego County)" section in the "New York Freshwater Fishing Guide" for details.

LOWER FLY SECTION
Bridge Pool

Located on the upstream side of the Altmar bridge, this hole is arguably the river's most famous because it marks the boundary between the regular fishing and fly-fishing only sections. Downstream of the bridge, you can fish with any legal rig and bait, and keep your catch. Above the bridge, fishing is restricted to catch and release with "traditional fly rod, fly reel, fly line and artificial fly." (Definitions and other information are available in the "Special Regulations for the Great Lakes Tributaries" in the state's freshwater fishing guide).

Gateway to the fly-fishing section, conveniently located right at the road, this spot always has anglers. Swinging streamers is the most popular and practical way to fish this pool, especially during the cold months. In summer, when anglers are few, "flea flicking," (matching the hatch), is also popular.

A FAS (Fishing Access Site) with a driftboat launch and parking for about 30 cars is located at the southeastern corner of the bridge.

Cemetery Pool

Skirting massive concrete blocks placed along the south bank at the second bend upstream of the Bridge Pool, this hole is named for the graveyard atop the hill.

This pool is best fished from the north bank. Unfortunately, that isn't always possible: the path starts at the northeastern corner of Bridge Street, in someone's front yard, and a posted sign usually blocks the path's entrance. Wading across the river from the upper end of the Altmar south FAS is risky because crossing back is impossible when the water is up—and it comes up quickly this close to the dam.

On the other hand, the south shore, the pool's deepest part, is lined with massive concrete blocks. A set of stairs on River Street, across from the church, make getting there easy. Since you'll be fishing deep current while standing above the water, dropping your fly almost straight down most of the time, it's good idea to hone your chuck-n'-duckin skills.

Stairs to the Cemetery Pool, fly-fishing section, Altmar.

UPPER FLY SECTION

The uppermost 0.5-mile of the fly-fishing section is upstream of the hatchery (fishing is prohibited on the river a short distance above and below the facility). The rule of thumb is the closer to the dam, the greater the number of fish. And this stretch comes through with flying colors. So many fish pack into this section, in fact, it's the main reason the stretch is restricted to catch and release. Its hot spots have some of the most spiritual names on the river.

The Point

Called the Last Chance Run by old-timers, this stretch of fast water rounds the bend below the Paradise Pool, turning left than right, and tumbles into a river-wide run.

Located several hundred yards downstream of the Steps (see below), this spot is a little out of the way. Beyond earshot of modern noises, requiring a degree of effort to get to, the Point doesn't exactly claim a lofty position on your average angler's list of the river's most popular hot spots. However, if you're looking for a rugged fishing experience with a hint of danger, this Point's remote location and towering cliff will fulfill your fantasy.

Since this spot requires crossing the river awfully close to the dam, it's wise to call Brookfield Power's Waterline to find out when the company plans to release water that day so you can be close to shore when it starts rising.

Get there from its intersection with NY 13 in Altmar by heading east on CR 22 for about a mile to the first FAS. Walk down the trail for a couple of hundred feet to the water—you'll be at the Steps. Head downstream, past the Paradise Pool (you'll know it when you see it), cross the river at the bend and continue downstream. The Point is at the next bend, where the river bears to the right.

Paradise Pool

Roughly 100 yards long by about 25 yards wide, averaging around 5 feet deep, this is one of the river's largest holes, and the biggest in the fly fishing section.

Crowned in whitewater, swept by a stiff current along the north bank, squeezed into a wide, shallow tailout, this hole is loaded with fishy-looking water. While it's been known to draw moderate fishing pressure during salmon season, and on sunny winter weekends, truth is, it's a little further from the road than most guys like and you'll be fishing alone most of the time.

Working nymphs at the head of the pool, letting them drift through the pool at the edge of the current, and swinging Wooly Buggers through the pockets at the head and tail, and swimming streamers through the current in the middle of the pool are good ways to attract chrome on sunny days, year-round. They'll hit on cloudy days, too, but not nearly as readily.

Dry flies dropped gently onto the hole's calm surfaces on summer mornings and will also hook a salmonid's interest. Patience is key; you just have to keep casting. Chances are you're coming close to fish— probably floating right over their heads, and they're not responding because you spooked them or they're just not hungry. Whatever the case, it can't last. All you can do is keep casting, gently. If you're quiet and move slowly, only when you have to, they'll forget you're there. Just keep casting the fly. Sooner or later it'll get in fish's face one time too many, and the beast'll try to kill it before it ruins the neighborhood.

The pool's only downside is creek minnows getting to your fly first, drowning your dries, mutilating your wets. While changing flies uses up a lot of valuable fishing time, seeing a chromer slurp a dry fly off the surface is priceless, well worth the effort.

Unfortunately, dry flies are only productive on balmy, sunny days. However, dead drifting an egg pattern or nymph along the edge of the current is productive just about anytime.

Get there from its intersection with NY 13 in Altmar by heading east on CR 22 for about 1.5 miles. Walk down the trail for a couple of hundred feet to the water—you'll be at the Steps. Continue downstream for a few hundred feet (you'll know it when you see it).

Steps

Formerly called the High Bank Pool, the name was changed to Steps after (take your pick):

Fran Verdoliva at the Steps, upper fly-fishing section.

A. Limestone steps were built into the cliff towering over the pool so fly anglers could get to the water without too much effort;

B. The pocketwater tumbling through the place resembles stairs;

C. The pockets look so promising, you'll be casting at every step . . .

This pool has always been popular with guys hardy enough to take on the challenge of getting to it. As recently as the summer of 2015, the river incessantly nibbled away at the steep south bank. The authorities put an end to the feast by building a wall of massive stone blocks at the head of the pool to shore up the bank, making fishing it easy.

One thing everyone familiar with the place agrees on is the Steps holds fish—lots of them.

Steelhead are always in the pool and the pockets below. You can realistically expect to hook one each time out.

A surprising number of bragging-size black bass also find the hole to their liking. Most anglers, feeling the Steps are too far away from the lake to draw its bass (they don't know bass), claim they slipped through the turbines or were thrown over the dam.

The steps are accessible by parking at the lower PAS on CR 22 (see directions above) and taking the trail straight in. When you reach the river, the Steps will be right there.

Purgatory Run

Spawned by the river coming together after being split by a short island, the colliding currents dig a relatively deep run punctuated with quiet pockets behind submerged boulders.

The south channel is the deepest and widest, and loads up with stockies in early summer.

Follow the above directions. When you come to the river, Purgatory will be just upstream.

Purgatory Run, upper fly-fishing section.

Hell's Gate

The uppermost rapids on the lower river, Hell's Gate pours out of the Snooze You Lose Pool at the bottom of the steep gorge that confines the stream for several hundred feet below the lower reservoir. Split by an island, the water tumbles, creating some very interesting pockets before leveling off briefly in a long, wide run on the southern channel, right at the end of the FAS trail. The southern arm is the widest and deepest.

Steelhead often hang tight to the island's bushy, undercut banks.

Snooze You Lose Pool

Also called the Upper Wire Hole because a wire stretching across the river bears a sign declaring fishing is prohibited further upstream, this hole is productive because it's at the end of the dam's tailrace, where the river breaks free of the gorge's confining walls, offering pockets at the edge of the rapids.

Park in the second PAS on CR 22 , take the path for a few hundred feet to the river and head upstream At the foot of the gorge you'll have to climb a steep bank, but a trail leads down to the water.

Appendix

Contacts

Douglaston Salmon Run
301 County Route 5
Pulaski, NY 13142
315-298-6672
www.douglastonsalmonrun.com

Fisheries Office
NYSDEC Region 7
1285 Fisher Ave.
Cortland, NY 13045-1090
607-753-3095

Salmon River Hatchery
2133 County Route 22
Altmar, NY 13302
315-298-5051

Spey Doctor (Spey Casting and Fly fishing School)
Walt Geryk
Hatfield, MA 01038
1-413-575-5421
www.speydoctor.com

Fishing Guides

Capt. Rick Miick
Dream Catcher Charters and Guide Service
247 Hadley Road
Sandy Creek, NY 13145
315-387-5920

McGrath & Assoc. Carp Angling Services
M.B. McGrath
378 Westbrook Hills Drive
Syracuse, NY 13215
315-469-5039

New York Fishtales
John Wisgo & Andrea Ulichny
322 Clark Road
Pulaski, NY 13142
315-298-3992
steelie11@frontiernet.net
www.nyfishtales.com

Outdoor Adventure Guide Service
Fred Kuepper
384 Johnson Road
Mexico, NY 13114
315-963-4095
fred@outdooradventureguide.net
www.outdooradventureguide.net

Pat Mahoney's Salmon River Outdoors, LLC
Patrick A. Mahoney
44 Bridge Street
Altmar, NY 13302
315-298-5108
www.salmonriveroutdoors.com

Paul's Guide Service
Paul Conklin
PO Box 351
Pulaski, NY 13142
315-298-3949
www.paulsguideservice.com

Salmon River Guide
Shane Thomas
1354 CR 48
Lacona, NY 13083
315-298-4530
www.salmonriverguide.com

Two Dog Outfitters
John F. Dembeck
1522 CR 3
Hannibal, NY 13074
315-564-6366
www.steelheadfishingoutfitters.com

UFly-fish.com Guide Service
James Zervos
74 Woodland Ave.
Binghamton, NY 13903
607-723-8082
www.uflyfish.com

Upstate Outfitters
Dick Redsicker
439 Centerville Rd.
Richland, NY 13144
315-569-3474

Tackle Shops

All Season Sports
3733 State Route 13
Pulaski, NY 13142
315-298-6433
www.allseasonssports.com

Fat Nancy's Tackle Shop
3750 State Route 13
Pulaski, NY 13142
877-801-3474
www.fatnancystackleshop.com

Malinda's Fly, Tackle and Spey Shop
3 Pulaski Street
Altmar, NY 13302
315-298-2993

Whitakers Sportshop & Motel
3707 NYS Route 13
Pulaski, NY 13142
315-298-6162
www.whitakers.com

Lodging

Fish On! Motel
19 Glen Avenue
Pulaski, NY 13142
315-298-3847
www.fishonmotel.com

Fox Hollow Lodge (campground, lodge and 8 cabins)
2740 State Route 13
Altmar, NY 13302
315-298-2876
www.foxhollowsalmonriverlodge.com

Salmon Acres Fishing Lodge
Thomas Rodda
3694 State Rt. 13
Pulaski, NY 13142
315-298-6173

Salmon River Outfitters
44 Bridge Street
Altmar, NY 13302
315-298-5442
www.salmonriveroutfittersny.com

Tailwater Lodge (pro shop, fly-fishing tackle)
52 Pulaski Street
Altmar, NY 13302
315-298-3434
www.TailwaterLodge.com

Public Access with Street Parking

Railroad Bridge Pool & Papermill Pool
(CR 2A, at the RR tracks)

Public Fishing Access with Parking

Pine Grove Boat Lunch
Pine Grove Road
Port Ontario, NY

Fishing Platform (Handicap Accessible)
NY 3
Port Ontario, NY

Black Hole
Riverview Drive
Pulaski, NY

Compactor Pool (DBL)
CR 2A
Pulaski, NY

Sportsman's Pool South
NY 13
Pineville, NY

Sportsmans Pool North
Centerville Road
Pineville, NY

Pineville (DBL)
NY 48
Pineville, NY

Trestle Hole South
NY 13
Altmar, NY

Trestle Hole North
Sheepskin Road
Pineville, NY

Ellis Cove
Bridge Street (Route 42)
Altmar, NY

Altmar (DBL)
Bridge Street (CR 52)
Altmar, NY

Driftboat Launches

Haldane Community Center
Maple Ave
Pulaski, NY

Lewis Street
Pulaski, NY

CR 2A
Pulaski, NY

CR 48
Pineville, NY

CR 52
Altmar, NY

Index